THE BEST THAT MONEY CAN'T BUY

BEYOND POLITICS, POVERTY, & WAR

BY JACQUE FRESCO

DATE DUE

Models, Illustrations & Photos
JACQUE FRESCO & ROXANNE MEADOWS

Model Designs
JACQUE FRESCO

GLOBAL CYBER-VISIONS
VENUS • FLORIDA

Publisher's Cataloging-in-Publication
(Provided by Quality Books, Inc.)
Fresco, Jacque, 1916-

    The best that money can't buy: beyond politics, poverty, & war / Jacque Fresco;
models; illustrations & photos, Jacque Fresco & Roxanne Meadows; model designs,
Jacque Fresco. — 1st ed.

    p. cm.
    ISBN: 0-9648806-7-9

    1. Social prediction. 2. Social change.
3. Technology — Social aspects.
4. Technological forecasting. I. Title

HM901.F74 2002   303.49
                              QBI01-201428

Published by Global Cyber-Visions
The Venus Project
21 Valley Lane
Venus, FL 33960
U.S.A.
Phone: 863-465-0321
Fax: 863-465-1928
http://www.thevenusproject.com
tvp@thevenusproject.com

This book was set in Adobe Centaur and Adobe Serpentine
Designed by Roxanne Meadows
Composition by Jonathan Pennell

International Standard Book Number: ISBN: 0-9648806-7-9
Library of Congress Catalog Number: 2001 135379
First Global Cyber-Visions Edition
10   9   8   7   6   5   4   3   2   1
Printed in the United States of America

ABOUT THE AUTHOR

JACQUE FRESCO

JACQUE FRESCO

Futurist **Jacque Fresco** is a forerunner in the field of Industrial Design and Human Factors Engineering. Over the years, he has conceived a vast array of creative and innovative designs and plans for such things as prefabricated houses, automobiles, electronic and medical equipment, and hundreds of commercial products and inventions. Included among his many inventions are a radical aircraft wing structure and technique for viewing three-dimensional motion pictures without the need for special viewing glasses. In addition, he has served as technical advisor for a number of motion pictures. His works and ideas have been presented on numerous television and radio talk shows throughout the

world, and articles about him have been featured in many national and international magazines and newspapers. Not only does he write and lecture about the future, but he actually lives in a future-oriented environment with his associate **Roxanne Meadows.** Together they have constructed a 25-acre research and development center in Venus, Florida where the future is unfolding. The Venus Project reflects the culmination of his life's work: the integration of the best of science and technology into a comprehensive plan for a new society based on human and environmental concern. It is a global vision of hope for the future of humankind in a technological age.

ROXANNE·MEADOWS

ACKNOWLEDGMENT

MY APPRECIATION GOES OUT TO MANY other contributors who have made this manuscript possible.

Steve Doll whose untiring efforts in helping to put the manuscript in order is deeply appreciated. He also offered many relevant editorial suggestions. Steve Doll with his years of experience in writing for many technical and social publications had an immediate grasp of the concepts described in this book.

Roxanne Meadows my dearest friend and companion helped with the organizing and layout of the book while making many helpful editorial suggestions. She has devoted her time and efforts for the past 25 years towards producing renderings, models, photographs, video editing, and constructing the buildings on the 25-acre site in Venus, Florida, while fulfilling highly challenging, full-time professional assignments of her own. Without her untiring patience, effort and dedication we would not have accomplished all that has been put forth towards the foundation of The Venus Project.

Susan Bottom and Marc Ponomareff, who have both assisted greatly in editing and revising the manuscript. I am also indebted to Marc for the final proofreading.

Angeles Philolias, whose untiring support and effort in presenting the concepts of The Venus Project to others has always been a source of inspiration and encouragement to both Roxanne and myself. Since his death in 2001 we have deeply missed him.

Arthur Shostak and Marco Scorcelletti for their support and help in attempting to get this manuscript published.

Sam Laurie for his many excellent editorial suggestions and support of the project.

Millard Deutsch has been very helpful in patiently typing as I dictated portions of this book.

I thank Ingrid and Dr. David Pon, and Wilson Hawthorn for their kindness and support of the project.

CONTENTS

VI THE BEST THAT MONEY CAN'T BUY

INTRODUCTION

IN OUR LONG AND EXPONENTIALLY GROWING LIST of technological achievements, perhaps none stand out so prominently as our forays beyond our own planet. With the dawn of the space age, astronauts and the public at large enjoy the unprecedented opportunity and privilege of viewing the earth in all of its colorful splendor and beauty, suspended against a backdrop of the black void of space. The narrative that usually accompanies this view is a whimsical one, reflecting the bond between earth and the billions of people who share this planet.

Global consciousness seems to inspire most of the space travelers who make these uplifting observations. For theirs has been an emotional, even spiritual experience. They seem to believe that this view from outer space cannot be interpreted as anything less than a grand global awakening to the realization that all the people who share our planet make up one, single community of brothers and sisters. They believe this viewpoint will help unite the nations of the world to build a peaceful future for humankind, both for the present generation and all those to follow.

Such has also been the preoccupation of many poets, philosophers, and writers through the ages who have bemoaned the artificiality of the borderlines that separate humankind. Despite the vision and hope of astronauts, poets, writers, and visionaries the reality is that nations are continuously at war with one another, while poverty and hunger still prevail in many places throughout the world, including the United States.

So far, not one astronaut who has arrived back on Earth with this cleansed social consciousness has offered a proposal to transcend the world's limitations and build a world where no national boundaries are represented. Each remains loyal to his/her particular nation-state, and will not venture beyond the boundaries of patriotism — "my country, right or wrong" — for to do so may risk their positions of prestige.

The problems we face in the world today are mostly of our own making. We must accept that the future depends upon us, the divine intervention of mythical characters in white robes who descend from the clouds or benign visitors from other worlds are illusions that cannot solve the problems of our modern world. The future of the world is our responsibility and depends upon the decisions that we make today. We are our own salvation or damnation. The shape and solutions of the future rely totally on the collective effort of all people working together.

Science and technology race ahead of us into the future, revealing new horizons in all areas. New discoveries and inventions appear at a rate never seen before in history. This rate of change will continue to increase in the years to come.

Unfortunately, the books and articles that attempt to describe the future have one foot rooted firmly in the past, while interpreting the future through today's concepts and technology. Most people feel comfortable with and are less threatened by this type of change. But they often recoil when confronted with proposals about changing the way they live. For this reason, when speaking of the future, very few explore or discuss changes to our social structure, much less our values. And yet that structure and those values reflect earlier times with different stresses and different levels of understanding. Any author who wants to publish wisely steers clear of such emotional and controversial issues. But we feel it is high time to step out of that box. In this book we will freely explore a new scenario of the future, one that is quite attainable and not the typical alternative of gloom and doom so often presented today.

Few can envision a social structure that enables everyone to attain a life style considered Utopian, even by today's standards — or, to take it even farther, that this lifestyle could be made available without working by the sweat of one's brow.

Yet consider the fact that, thanks to our labor-saving machines and other technological advances, the lifestyle of the middle class person today far exceeds anything that even kings of the past could have experienced.

Since the onset of the machine age, humankind has maintained a sort of love/hate relationship with its mechanical progeny. We may like what the machines do for us, but we don't like what we perceive they are doing *to* us. They take away our means of making a living, and consequently our sense of purpose, instilled through thousands of years of human enterprise in which hand labor has been the primary means of meeting human needs.

Many of us fear that as machines become more and more complex and sophisticated, and our dependence on them grows, we give over much of our own independence and become as they — passionless, unfeeling automatons whose sole purpose in life is to work, work, work. Such people fear that, eventually, these mechanical children could develop minds and wills of their own and enslave humanity to do their soulless bidding.

Many fear that our values and behavior will change to meet the dictates of uniformity, and that humanity will lose those very qualities which make us distinctly human. The purpose of this book is to explore other visions and possibilities for the future that nurture human growth and achievements as the primary goal of a healthy society. We propose to discuss the many options and roles the individual will play in the unfolding of this cybernated age, an age in which our world is rebuilt by prodigious machines and governed by computers.

Most writers of the twentieth century who attempted to present a vision of the future, blinded either by national ego or self-centeredness, failed to grasp the significance and meaning of the methods of science as they might be applied to the social system.

Although it may appear that the thrust of this book is the technology of the future, our major concern is the effect a totally cybernated world would have on humanity and on the individual. Of course, no one can really predict the future with precision. There are simply too many variables beyond our comprehension. New inventions, natural and man-made disasters, or new, uncontrollable diseases may radically alter the course of civilization. While we cannot confidently predict the future, we will most surely live it. Every action and decision we make — or don't — ripples into the future. For the first time, we have the capability, the technology, and the knowledge to direct those ripples.

When applied in a humane direction, the primary directive of the emerging, cybernated age could be the synthesizing of technology and cybernetics into a workable and human synergy for the people of all nations. It could achieve a world free of hunger, war and poverty — a world humanity failed to achieve throughout history. But if civilization continues on its present course we will simply repeat the same cycle of inadequacy all over again.

Applying what we already know to enhance the quality of all human life on earth could at the same time — indeed, must — protect the environment and the symbiotic process of living systems. It is now mandatory that we intelligently rearrange human affairs to comply with available resources. The proposals of this book are about the limitless, untapped potentials and the future application of new technologies where our health, intellect and well-being are involved, not only in the material sense but also with a deep concern for one another. Only in this way can science and technology support a meaningful and humane civilization.

Many of us who think seriously about the future of human civilization are familiar with stark scenarios of the new millennium in a world of growing chaos and disorder, of soaring populations and dwindling natural resources. Emaciated children cry out to us from decayed cities and villages, their mouths agape over bellies swollen from malnutrition and wasting disease. In more affluent areas, the problems associated with urban sprawl, air and water pollution and escalating crime take their toll on the quality of life, even for those who consider themselves sufficiently removed from these conditions. But even the financially wealthy exist at a tremendous disadvantage with their inability to grasp the damage of technology applied without social concern.

With the advances in science and technology over the last two hundred years, one may well ask: does it have to be this way? There is no question that the human application of science and technology can carry us with confidence and assurance into the future. What is needed is a change in our sense of direction and purpose. Our main problem is a lack of understanding of what it means to be human and the full realization that we human beings are not separate from nature. Our values, beliefs, and behavior are as much a part of the natural law as any other natural process. We are all an integral part of the chain of life.

In this book, we present an alternative vision for a sustainable new world civilization unlike any social system that has gone before. Although this vision is highly compressed, it is based upon years of study and experimental research. We call for a straightforward redesign of our culture, in which the age-old inadequacies of war, poverty, hunger, debt, and unnecessary human suffering are viewed not only as avoidable, but also as totally unacceptable. Anything less simply results in a continuation of the same catalog of problems inherent in the present system.

CHAPTER 1

A DESIGN FOR THE FUTURE

THE FUTURE IS FLUID. Each act, each decision, each development adds new possibilities and eliminates others. But the future is ours to direct. In older times, change came so slowly that generations passed with minimal impact on the daily business of surviving. Social structures and cultural norms remained static for centuries.

In the last fifty to a hundred years technology and social change accelerated to such an extent, governments and corporations now consider change management a core process.

Hundreds of books address technological change, business process management, human productivity, and environmental issues. The best of our universities offer advanced degrees in public and environmental affairs. Almost all overlook the major element in all these systems — human beings and their social structures and culture. Technology, policy and automation do nothing until humans accept them and apply them to their daily lives. This book offers a blueprint to consciously fuse all these elements to create a sustainable future for all our planetary inhabitants, as well as fundamental changes in the way we regard ourselves, one another and our world. This can be accomplished through the infusion of technology and cybernetics applied with human and environmental concern to secure, protect, and encourage a more humane world for all people.

How may such a prodigious task be accomplished? First, we need a current survey of all our available planetary resources. All the discussion in the world on what is scarce and what is plentiful is just so much talk until we actually measure our resources. We must first baseline what we have around the world. This information must be compiled to ascertain the possible parameters for *humanizing* social and technological development. This may be accomplished through the use of large-scale, computer-based processors that will assist us in defining the most humane and appropriate way to manage environmental and human affairs. This is essentially the function of government. With computers able to process trillions of bits of information per second, existing technologies can far exceed the human capacity for processing the necessary information and arriving at equitable and sustainable decisions involving the development and distribution of physical resources. With this potential we may eventually surpass the need for political decisions made on the basis of power and advantage.

Eventually, with artificial intelligence, money may become irrelevant, particularly in a high-energy civilization in which a material abundance eliminates our belief in the concept of scarcity valuation. We have arrived at a time when new innovations in the methods of science and technology can provide abundance to all the world's people. It is no longer necessary to consciously withhold efficiency by planned obsolescence, or to utilize an old and outworn monetary system

Although many of us like to consider ourselves forward-thinkers, we still cling tenaciously to all the values of the old monetary system. We accept unthinkingly a system that breeds inefficiencies and actually encourage the creation of shortages.

For example, while many concerns over environmental destruction and the misuse of technology are justified, many environmentalists draw bleak scenarios of the future based on present day methodologies and shortages. They view environmental destruction from the only point of reference they have to work with — existing technologies used wastefully and irresponsibly, primarily to support outmoded concepts and the economic imperative of sales turnover and customer appeal. Although we concede that technological development has been misdirected, the vast benefits far outweigh the negative factors involved. Only the most diehard environmental activist would turn his back on the many advances made toward the elevation of the human condition in areas such as medicine, communications, power generation, and food production.

If human civilization is to endure, it must eventually outgrow the need for conspicuous waste of time, effort, and natural resources. One area in which we may witness this is in architecture. Resource conservation must be incorporated into our structures.

With a conscious and intelligent application of today's science and technology to human and environmental concern, we can recreate the wetlands and enhance the symbiotic process between the elements of nature. This was not attainable in earlier times.

While many urban centers grapple with the daunting task of retrofitting new, more efficient technologies into their existing infrastructures, these efforts continue to fall far short of the potentials of technology. In addition to rebuilding our thought patterns, much of our physical infrastructure — industrial plants, buildings, waterways, power systems, production and distribution processes, and transportation systems — must be reconstructed from the ground up. Only then may we use our technology to overcome resource deficiencies and provide universal abundance.

If we are genuinely concerned about the environment and our fellow human beings, and if we really want to put an end to territorial disputes, war, crime, poverty, hunger, and many of the other problems that confront all nations today, the intelligent use of science and technology offers us the tools with which we can strive toward a new direction — one that could serve the well-being of all people, and not just a select few.

The purpose of all this technology is to ultimately free people from repetitive and boring jobs and allow humans to truly experience the fullness of human relationships, which has been denied to so many for so long. This will call for a basic realignment of the way we think about what makes us human. Our times demand the declaration of the world's resources as the common heritage of all people.

Perhaps at the passing of the next hundred years, future historians may look back on our present civilization as a transition point from the dark ages of ignorance, superstition, and social insufficiency — much as we view the world of a few hundred years ago. If we arrive at a saner world in which the maximum human potential is cultivated in every person, our descendants will not understand how our world of billions of human beings produced only one Louis Pasteur, one Edison, one Tesla, one Salk, and why great achievements in our age were the products of a relative few.

In looking ahead to the next millennium, and back to the dimmest memories of human civilization, we see the thoughts, dreams, and visions of humanity are limited by a system of scarcity. We are all products of a culture of deficiency, a culture that expects each confrontation and most activities to end with a winner and a loser, and funding restricts even technological development that has the potential to liberate humanity from its past insufficiencies.

We no longer have the luxury of such primitive thinking. There are other ways of looking at our lives and the world that we live in. Either we learn to live together in full cooperation or we will create our own extinction. To fully understand and appreciate this coming age, we must first understand the relationship between creation and creator: the machine and, as of this writing, that most marvelous of mechanisms — the human being.

CHAPTER 2

CHANGING VALUES
IN AN EMERGING CULTURE

ANY ATTEMPT TO DEPICT THE FUTURE DIRECTION of civilization must include a straightforward description of the probable evolution of our culture without embellishment, propaganda, or national interest. We must reexamine our traditional habits of thought if we wish to avoid the consequences of not preparing for the future. It is unfortunate that most of us try to shape or envision this future within our present social framework, attempting to maintain values and traditions that reflect the past. Such superficial changes tend to perpetuate the problems of today. The challenges we face today cannot be answered by antiquated notions and values that are no longer relevant.

Imagine a new planet with the same carrying capacity as the earth, and that you are free to design a new direction for society on this planet. You can choose any shape or form. The only limitation imposed upon you is that your proposed, alternative social design must correspond to the carrying capacity of that planet. This new planet has more than adequate arable land, clean air and water, and an abundance of untapped resources. This is your planet. You can rearrange the entire social order to correspond to whatever you consider the best of all possible worlds. Not only does this include environmental modification, but also human factors, interpersonal relationships and the reordering of education.

This need not be complicated. It can be an uncluttered approach, unburdened by any past or traditional considerations, religious or otherwise. This is a prodigious project, perhaps calling for the introduction of many disciplines, applied to the way the inhabitants of your planet conduct their lives — always keeping in mind for whom and for what ends this social order is designed. Feel free to transcend present realities and reach for new and inventive ideas with which to shape your world of the future. An exciting exercise, isn't it? What we propose is nothing more nor less than applying that analysis to our planet.

To prepare for the future we must be willing to test newer concepts. This means that we must acquire enough information to evaluate these concepts, unlike the travelers who go to a foreign land and immediately compare everything with their own hometown. To understand people of another place we must set aside our expectations of behavior, lay aside the value patterns to which we have become accustomed.

If you believe today's values and virtues are absolute and ultimate, and reflect the final value systems for all times and all civilization, then you may find our projection of the future shocking and unacceptable. We must feel and think as freshly as possible about the almost limitless possibilities and combinations of life patterns humankind may explore for attaining even higher levels of intelligence and fulfillment in the future.

Although such individuals as Plato, Edward Bellamy, H.G. Wells, Karl Marx, and Howard Scott have all made some attempts to plan a new civilization, the established social order inevitably considered them impractical dreamers with Utopian designs that ran contrary to the innate elements of human nature. Arrayed against these social pioneers was a formidable status quo composed of vested interests that were comfortable with the way things were, and a populace at large that, out of years of indoctrination, went unthinkingly along for the ride. These were the millions of unappointed guardians of the status quo. The outlook and philosophy of the leaders were consistent with their positions of differential advantage.

In spite of the vast advances in the human condition achieved through the process of objective scientific investigation, and the breaking down of long-standing fears and superstitions regarding the world we live in, the world today is still not a reasonable place. Many attempts to make it so have failed due to selfish individual and national interests. Deeply rooted cultural norms that assume someone must lose for someone else to gain (scarcity at it most basic) still dictate most of our decisions. For example, we still cling to the concept of competition and inadequate compensation for people's efforts, i.e. minimum wage, when such tactics are no longer applicable or appropriate to our capabilities and resources, never mind their effect on human dignity and any possible elevation of the human condition.

At this turning point in our civilization, we find our difficulties compounded by the fact that too many of us still wait for someone, a messiah perhaps, the elusive "they", or an extraterrestrial to save us. The irony behind this is that, as we wait for someone to do it for us, we give over to them our freedom of choice and movement. We react rather than act toward events and issues.

The future is our responsibility and significant change will most probably not take place until the vast majority of the world's people lose confidence in their dictators and their elected officials' ability to solve problems. It will most likely take an economic catastrophe of unprecedented proportions resulting in an enormous amount of human suffering to bring about true social change. Unfortunately, this does not guarantee that the change will be beneficial.

In times of conflict between nations, we still default to answering a perceived threat with a threat, developing weapons of mass destruction and training people to use them against other people whom we regard as our enemies. Many of our so-called social reformers tried to solve our problems of crime within the framework of the monetary system by building more prisons and enacting new laws, i.e. gun legislation and "three times and you're out" provisions in an attempt to govern crime and violence. This has accomplished very little, yet requests for additional funding to build more prisons and hire more policemen fare far better in legislatures and voting referendums than do pleas for additional education funding or aid to the poor. Somehow in the era of true plenty, we have meanly adopted national approval for punishment as an answer to all problems. One symptom of insanity would surely be the repeating of the same mistake, over and over again — each time expecting a different outcome. Our society is, in this sense, truly insane.

The Manhattan Project developed the first atomic device to be used against human populations — and launched the most intensive and dangerous weapons build-up in history. The Manhattan Project was also one of the largest and best-financed projects ever undertaken. If we are willing to spend that amount of money, resources and human lives in times of war, we must ask why we don't commit equal resources to improving the lives of everyone and anticipating the humane needs of the future? The same energies that went into the Manhattan Project could be channeled to improve and update our way of life, and to achieve and maintain the optimal symbiotic relationship between nature and humankind.

If our system continues without the appropriate modification and environmental and social concern we will eventually face an inevitable economic and social breakdown of our outworn monetary and political system. When this occurs the established government will most likely enact a state of emergency or marshal law to prevent total chaos. I do not advocate this but without the suffering of millions of people it may be almost impossible to shake our complacency with our current way of life.

OUT OF THE DARK AGES

Many scientists participating in the space program face different challenges. For example, space scientists must develop new ways of eating in outer space. Astronauts' clothing must withstand the vacuum of outer space, enormous temperature differentials and radiation — yet remain light in weight and permit a high degree of flexibility. This new clothing design even calls for the possible development of self-repairing systems. Their challenge is to conceive of common items in completely new ways. In space, for example, clothing no longer functions as just body covering and adornment. It becomes a mini-habitat.

The space age represents a prime example of the relentless search for newer and better ways of doing things. As scientists continue to probe toward the limits of our universe, they must generate newer techniques and technologies for unexplored frontiers and never-before-encountered environments. If they cling tenaciously to the concepts of their earlier training, our explorations will fail. Had our ancestors refused to accept new ideas, the physical sciences would have progressed little beyond the development of the covered wagon.

Many young engineers, scientists, and architects face this dilemma. Bold and creative, they exit institutions of higher learning and step out into the world eager for change. They set out with great enthusiasm but are often beaten back and slowed by the established institutions and self-appointed guardians of tradition. Occasionally, some men and women break away from traditional concepts and set out as innovators. They meet such tremendous resistance by antiquated building codes and other restrictions that their daring concepts are soon reduced to mediocrity.

Many of the dominant values that shape our present society are still medieval. The myth that we live in an enlightened age or an age of reason really has little basis. We are overwhelmed with valid information concerning ourselves and our planet, most of which we have no inkling of how to apply. Most of our customs and modes of behavior are locked in the dungeons of the mental Dark Ages and have been handed down to us.

It was difficult for early forms of life to crawl out of the primordial slime without dragging some of it with them. So it is with any entrenched value system. The most appropriate place for traditional concepts should be in a museum or in books about the history of civilization.

The most significant changes of the twenty-first century will reveal what most people never suspected, that the majority of us have the potential of people such as Leonardo da Vinci, Alexander Graham Bell and Madam Curie, if raised in an environment that encourages genuine individuality and creativity. This includes all the other characteristics believed to be the product of a special and privileged heredity of great men and women.

Even in today's so called democratic society considerably less than 4% of the world's people have supplied us with the scientific and artistic advances that sustain the operation of the world's social system.

SHAPING HUMAN VALUES

The human beings of the future, although similar in appearance, could differ considerably in their outlook, values and mindset. The social orders of the past that have prevailed into the twenty-first century consistently sought to generate loyalty and conformity to established institutions as the only means to sustain a workable society. Countless laws — usually passed after a misdeed has occurred — have been enacted in an attempt to govern the conduct of people. Those who do not conform are ostracized or imprisoned.

During the preceding eras of social change, many social reformers and those disdainfully called agitators by their detractors were not generally angry, maladjusted individuals. They were often people with a deeper sensitivity and concern for the needs of others, who envisioned a better life for all people. Among these we may count the abolitionists, advocates for woman's suffrage and child labor laws, those who practiced non-violent resistance to oppression, and so-called "freedom fighters" everywhere.

Today we accept without question most of the achievements of these reformers, who faced violent opposition, imprisonment, ridicule and even death from vested interests and the established order. Unfortunately most people are completely unaware of the identities of those individuals who helped pave the way toward social enlightenment.

Most of our parks have statues of warriors and statesman, while any monuments to the really great social innovators are rare indeed. Possibly when the history of the human race is finally written, it will be told from the viewpoint of individuals who found themselves in an alien and primitive culture and sought change in a world with a built-in tenacity to maintain things as they are.

Conformity on the part of the population makes the control of society much easier for its leaders. Our leaders emphasize the freedom that democracy provides while supporting an economic structure that imprisons it citizens under more and more debt. They proclaim that all have the opportunity to work their way to the top of the ladder through the relentless effort of individual initiative and incentive. To appease those who work hard and do not achieve the good life, religion is there to assure them that if not in this life they will obtain it in the next.

Our habits of thought and conduct reflect the effectiveness of the constant and unrelenting propaganda of radio, television, publications, and most other media. They are so effective that the average citizen is not even insulted when being categorized as a consumer — as if a citizen's sole worth to society was as a user of goods. These patterns, however, are gradually being modified and challenged by the silent infusion of the Internet and the World Wide Web.

Most people today simply expect that our televisions, computers, communications systems, and methods of production and delivery of services — even our concepts of work and reward — will continue to improve without any disruption or distress within our present value systems. But this is not necessarily so. Our dominant values with their emphasis on competition and scarcity limit our continued progress.

The most disruptive period of a transition from an established social order to an emergent system result when people are not prepared emotionally or intellectually to adjust to change. People cannot simply erase all the belief systems and habits acquired during previous times, which they associate with self-identification. Sudden changes in values without the necessary preparation will cause many of the unprepared to lose their sense of identity and purpose, isolating them from a society they believe has passed them by. Another limiting factor that prevents people from properly evaluating alternative social proposals is the lack of understanding of basic scientific principles and the factors responsible for shaping culture and our behavior.

The conflicts today with our fellow human beings are over opposing values. If we manage to arrive at a saner future civilization, the conflicts will be against problems common to all humans. In a vibrant and emergent culture, rather than having conflicts between nations, the challenges we will face will be overcoming scarcity, restructuring damaged environments, creating innovative technologies, increasing agricultural yield, improving communications, building communications between nations, sharing technologies, and living a meaningful life.

WORK AND THE NEW LEISURE

From early civilizations to the present day most humans had to work to earn a living. Most of our attitudes about work may be a carry-over from these earlier times. In the past (and still in many low-energy cultures), it was necessary for people to fetch water and carry it to their dwelling places. They gathered wood to prepare fires for heating and cooking, and fuel to burn in their lamps. It would have been very difficult — and still is for some — to imagine a time when water would rush forth in their own dwelling with the turn of a handle; to press a button for instant light would have seemed to be within the realm of magic. People of ancient times probably wondered what they would do with their time if they did not have to engage in these burdensome tasks that were so necessary to sustain their lives. In most developed countries of the world today tasks that were once so vital to a people's very survival are no longer necessary, thanks to modern technology.

Today people attend schools to acquire the marketable skills that enable them to earn a living in the "work-a-day" world. Recently, this cherished belief that one must work to earn a living is being challenged. Working for a living to supply the necessities of life may soon be irrelevant due to the ability of modern technology to provide most of these needs. As a result, many jobs have gone the way of the iceman and the elevator operator. Perhaps we have a semantic problem with the word "work." The idea of "freedom from work" should be equated with the elimination of repetitive and boring tasks that hold back our intellectual growth. Most jobs, from blue-collar assembly workers to professionals, entail repetitive and uninteresting tasks. All human beings possess a tremendous, untapped potential that they will finally be able to explore when they are free of the burden of having to work to earn a living.

At present there are no plans in government or industry to make the necessary economic adjustments to deal with the issue of the displacement of people by automated technology. It is no longer the repetitive work of just the laborers that cybernation is able to phase out but also many other vocations and professions. Engineers, technicians, scientists, doctors, architects, artists, and actors will all have their roles altered, sometimes drastically. Therefore, it is absolutely imperative that we explore alternatives to improve our social constructs, beliefs, and quality of life to secure and sustain a future for all people.

CHAPTER 3

LANGUAGE OF RELEVANCE

OF THE MANY OLD, ENTRENCHED BARRIERS to positive change, communication has proven the most intractable. The languages of the majority of the world's peoples evolved over periods of centuries, through ages of scarcity, superstition and social insufficiency, and are continuing to evolve. However, the current state of language often lends itself more to ambiguity and uncertainties where important issues are at stake, rather than to a precise and universally intelligible means of conveying knowledge. It is often extremely difficult for the average person — and even those considered above average, including leaders of nations — to share ideas with others whose worldview may be at considerable variance with their own. Also, due to semantic differences and our different experiences, words have varying shades of meaning.

What will happen should we make contact with an alien civilization, when we haven't been able to make contact with our fellow human beings? We are not ready for that. We haven't yet learned to resolve international differences by peaceful methods. Unfortunately we live in a world today where peace is simply a pause between wars.

Even in the United States, supposedly the most technologically advanced country in the world, we lack a unified, definitively stated direction. And so our policies and goals are fragmented, contradictory. The Democrats cannot communicate meaningfully with the Republicans. Elsewhere, the Israelis oppose the Arabs, the Irish Catholics clash with the Irish Protestants, the Serbs with the Muslims. Everywhere there is interracial disharmony, the inability of husbands and wives to communicate with each other or their children, labor and management strife, the communists differing with the capitalists.

How then in the name of sanity could we hope to establish any sort of meaningful level of communication with an alien civilization, with beings possessing the intelligence and social coherence to develop technologies far in advance of our own? Perhaps from the aliens' point of view, they might well wonder whether there really is intelligent life on earth.

Most world leaders seek to achieve greater communication and understanding among the nations of the world. Unfortunately, their efforts to achieve that goal have met with little success. One reason for this is that each comes to the table determined to achieve the optimal position of advantage for their own national interest. We talk a great deal about global development and global cooperation. But the "global" in each case reflects the individual nation's interests and not those of all the people of the world.

In addition we are trapped within old ways of looking at our world. While most of us agree change is necessary, many limit the extent of change if it threatens their position of advantage, just as on a personal basis they seek change in others, rather than themselves.

Many of us lack the skills to truly communicate logically when we are emotionally invested in an outcome. If a person or group of people has difficulty in communicating a point in question, rather than seek clarification they raise their voices. If this does not produce the desired effect, they may incorporate profanity or intimidating language. If this still does not work, they may resort to physical violence, punishment or deprivation as a means of achieving what they consider to be the desired behavior. Unfortunately, in some instances deprivation of the means of earning a living has been, and continues to be, used.

These tactics have never contributed to a heightened level of understanding. In fact, many of these attempts to control behavior actually increased violence and drove the parties farther apart. It would probably be difficult for a future historian to understand why the language of science and technology was not incorporated into everyday communication.

THE LANGUAGE OF SCIENCE

Ambiguity may enable lawyers, preachers and politicians to function, but it falls short in accomplishing the tasks of building bridges, dams, power projects, flying machines, or enterprises involving space travel. For these precise functions, we need the language of science. Even amid this labyrinth of ambiguity, this much more serviceable language is coming into use throughout the world, particularly in the technologically advanced countries.

If communication is to improve, we need a language with a high degree of physical correlation with the environment and human needs. We already have such a language shared by the science and technology communities and easily understood by many of the world's nations.

In other words, it is possible to establish a coherent means of communications without ambivalence. If we apply the same methods used in the physical sciences to psychology, sociology and the humanities, a great deal of unnecessary conflict could be resolved. In such disciplines of science as engineering, mathematics, chemistry, and other technical fields we have examples of the nearest thing to a descriptive universal language that leaves little room for individual interpretation.

For instance, if a blueprint for an automobile were to be given to any technologically developed society anywhere in the world, regardless of their political or religious beliefs the finished product would be very similar to that in other areas receiving the same blueprint.

The language used today by the average person is inadequate for resolving conflicting ideas, whereas the language of science is relatively free of the ambiguities and conflict prevalent in our everyday, emotion-driven language. It was deliberately *designed* — as opposed to evolving through centuries of cultural change — as the most appropriate way to state a problem in terms that are verifiable and readily understood by most people.

Many of the great technical strides made in the present world would have been unattainable without this type of improved communication. Without a common, descriptive language, we would have been unable to prevent diseases, increase crop yields, talk over thousands of miles, or build bridges, dams, transport systems, and the many other technological marvels of this computerized age.

Unfortunately, the same does not hold true for conversational language. Any attempt to discuss or evaluate newer concepts in social design is greatly limited by our habit of comparing newer concepts to existing systems and beliefs.

IT'S A SEMANTIC JUNGLE OUT THERE

Utopian ideals have almost certainly existed as long as humans have dealt with problems and reflected upon a world free of them — or at least having only a minimal amount. The framers of scriptural references to Eden, Plato's *Republic*, H. G. Wells' *Shape of Things to Come*, and such concepts as socialism, communism, democracy, and the ultimate expression of bliss, Heaven, have all shared this Utopian dream. All attempts at creating such a world seem to have fallen far short of their vision, possibly because the dreamers and visionaries who have projected their Utopian concepts did so mostly within the framework and values of their existing culture. The language that they used was limited and subject to a wide range of individual interpretations.

When we read and discuss new ideas, the information is automatically filtered through previous experiences and patterns of associative memory. In many instances what we end up with is something other than the designers intended. Unfortunately we live in a linguistic and semantic jungle. The use of language that we inherited is insufficient and lacks the fundamental means whereby ideas can be shared.

To cite an historical example, when presented with the possibility of the transition from conventional aircraft configuration to the flying wing concept during World War II (now employed very effectively in the B-I Stealth bomber), most people first noticed the absence of the tail assembly. This new configuration, so far removed from the conventional, made them uncomfortable and their reactions were generally hostile. Even technical people questioned the lack of stability believed to be inherent in the flying wing.

They responded with doubt and hostility. Had they used the appropriate language of investigation, they would instead have asked the designer how he intended to overcome the limiting factors in the earlier designs. The designer would have responded by presenting new ideas through design specifications and — better yet — working models of the subject matter under discussion.

To continue a discussion of the redesign of a culture — not Utopian, but simply in accordance with the knowledge and resources we have at hand — we must learn to outgrow our egos in exchange for constructive dialogue rather than debate. In addition we must be capable of stating problems and proposing alternative solutions clearly and succinctly, in ways that are not subject to distortion of meaning or misunderstanding, even if these solutions are radically opposed to the accepted norms.

CHANGING LANGUAGE

Language evolves along with a people and their culture. With the development of newer technologies our everyday language changes accordingly. But today our technology and culture is so pervasive, we need a much more uniform meaning throughout the world. This would be similar to mathematics in that it avoids semantic differences in interpretation. This new language could have symbols designed for a close approximation with real events in the physical world. An advanced descriptive language will most likely eventually be designed by artificial intelligence and continuously updated to remain relevant to existing circumstances and new situations.

Perhaps the future language may transcend words as we know them to become a series of sounds sequentially arranged to produce a desired response in others. *Language is an attempt to control behavior through the transfer of information, valid, invalid, or even irrelevant to the situation.*

Perhaps as it becomes essential that clarification of goals be stated precisely, our language will undergo considerable modification. The refinement and enlargement of our present language cannot be explained within the bounds of our existing temporary idiom usage. It must evolve and undergo constant refinement, while increasing the scope of meaning before it becomes an effective means of communication between people.

It is unfortunate that Guttenberg invented the printing press before the English alphabet and spelling had become stabilized. Many of our language's idiosyncrasies still endure from those early days of experimentation. No sophistication of phrasing or vocabulary alter the fact that different words, and even the same words in different sequences, have so many possible interpretations that their semantic connotations differ from sender to receiver — and from that receiver to others. Our language has an amazing richness and flexibility that easily accommodates change. But when the exception is the rule, clear communication is a challenge.

In the future, people assisted by computers could initiate a language that will offer closer areas of understanding and a much simpler structure with fewer guttural sounds. For example, a series of signals combining acoustical, optical, olfactory, and teletactile electronic patterns will tell a story in seconds, rather than in many sentences or pages.

Such a methodology is not far removed from that which enables fish to find the Oronoco River thousands of miles away from their starting point without ever having been there before. Fish have receptors that sense the earth's magnetic field, which to a large extent shapes their behavior. In a like manner, imprinting in a bird probably elicits the nest-building pattern. When our technologies are more closely aligned with natural law, airplanes could use geomagnetic fields for navigation, just as these fields may serve as guides to migratory patterns for birds.

A clearer, more efficient means of communicating ideas and experiences would result in a more exact expression for human verbal interaction. It could open an entirely new area of science — a science of significance and meaning. The introduction of a refined language could result in a rearrangement of the associative systems in the human brain, resulting in greater understanding and reduction in conflict.

BRIDGES OVER TROUBLED WORDS

Taken in its common context, a myth is a concept or tale unsubstantiated by factual proof. For our purposes, the word denotes a non-referential method for stating problems. In this context, the author considers the matter of resolving conflicts on the basis of mutual "understanding" a myth.

For example, the possibility of members of the Jewish faith resolving the conflict of the Nazi point of view through the free exchange of views is extremely remote, if not non-existent. The same difficulties may be encountered by a well-educated African-American attempting to resolve conflict with a white supremacist organization, or a scientist sharing the Darwinian theory of evolution with religious fundamentalists. This is largely due to the fact that human beings, as yet, are not rational beings in any sense of the word.

Our values pertaining to right, and wrong, good and bad, are the byproducts and operating procedures of older social systems. For example, such slogans and catch phrases as "God is on our side", "Think American", "successful person", "well adjusted", "mature outlook", and "sharing ideas", are all statements and assessments relative to the culture in which they originated. If we genuinely hope to bridge differences, we need a much more precise language and a mindset more open to new ideas.

Actually, there is no sharing of relevant values — no communication at all — if the parties either have no common starting point or are unwilling/unable to conceive of any experience outside their own. If a person believes that it is impossible to build a flying machine, the builder of the flying machine cannot share any knowledge relative to the idea because the doubting party offers no inquiry as to how it can be accomplished. He or she has already dismissed it in their mind.

How, then, in a culture-bound society with equally limited language and ideals, can we introduce concepts of a future society with values far removed from the present? How can we orient the listener to new concepts for which, even if they have the desire to learn, they have no point of reference in their experience and thinking ability?

For the most part, we live in a perpetual "show me" state. When Nikola Tesla first introduced the concept of the wireless, there was no common understanding of the methods and dynamics of wireless transmission. Instead, Tesla oriented the uninformed through a demonstration of the working processes.

In like manner films, books, seminars, videos and ultimately a first working prototype of a new city system based on a new social direction will be essential to demonstrate the validity of our proposals.

CHAPTER 4

FROM SUPERSTITION TO SCIENCE

THE CHALLENGES WE FACE TODAY CANNOT BE RESOLVED by antiquated notions and values that are no longer relevant. Unfortunately we tend to support the basic values and traditions that reflect the past, without questioning their appropriateness to the present or the future. The more superficial the changes, the more things remain the same. For us to think creatively about our future and examine our traditional habits of thought, we must become better informed. We must look at other alternatives objectively rather than trying to fit the future into our present social mold.

Even today, millions of people throughout the civilized world still worship many different gods and fear demons, while others tend to placate their gods with incantations, sacrifices, adulation and flattery. Still others use astrological charts and pendulums for arriving at decisions. Even many of the most popular newspapers feature a column on astrology, while television and radio airwaves are filled with psychic problem solvers. A noted psychic recently proclaimed we would be surprised at just how many of the important decisions of running our country were in the hands of soothsayers and charlatans.

Until the discipline of scientific inquiry came of age, human beings could not comprehend their relationship to the physical world, so they invented their own explanations. These explanations tended to be simple and some harmful resulting in religious rituals superstitions, astrology, numerology, fortune telling, etc. Millions of people still accept and follow these ancient beliefs.

It is not that scientists are closed-minded regarding these issues, their standards for accepting such ideas simply require a much more rigorous and sophisticated method of inquiry. The difference between the scientist and the metaphysician is that the scientist asks a question and engages in experiments to determine the nature of the physical world; part of this process requires that the experiments be verified by others who must get the same result. In contrast, the metaphysicians fabricate answers that are pleasing to them and which require no verification, a process involving little or no effort.

When we consider the extent to which metaphysicians rely on this unverifiable information for direction, it is ironic to see them immediately surrender their lofty intuitive and spiritual interpretations of worldly things when it comes to their daily lives. When purchasing property, for example, they measure exactly how many square feet are being exchanged for a given sum of money. When purchasing a new automobile, they ask how many miles per gallon the car will deliver, or the precise amount of fuel needed to travel a given distance.

In fact, most of our daily living is based upon the application of scientific principles. As B.F. Skinner would say, "intuitive feelings may tickle the cockles of a poet's heart", but this does nothing to enhance our knowledge of the physical world. What makes a person feel good or appeals to one's emotions does not necessarily add to one's understanding of our world.

Throughout history life for most people has been a perpetual struggle against a great many problems: finances, health, personal safety, security, starvation, and a myriad of others. Failing to find a safe haven in a world in which many are resigned to the consequences of our original sin, theologians created the concept of a distant Heaven, a place of eternal bliss and a limitless abundance of warmth and love, where all of the people are free of destitution, greed, lust, the need for money and all the other afflictions that plagued humankind for centuries.

Of course, to qualify for entrance into this world of eternal bliss, one must die and, prior to that, demonstrate impeccable earthly behavior, engage in constant prayer to an intermediary for forgiveness for one's transgressions.

Others seek to attain this end while still on an earthly plane through meditation or renunciation of the material world. By this means they claim they will be able to experience Nirvana. Although it is true this form of meditation will alter their associative memory and develop the necessary procedure for fulfilling their hopes, dreams and wishes, the attainment of this state takes place only in their own mind. This procedure for inducing wish fulfillment and dreams of unique individual fantasies often makes it extremely difficult for people to know the difference between the physical world and their created fantasies.

People will continue to search for answers to these universal and perplexing problems. But to find meaningful answers, one must first know the appropriate questions to ask. People pose questions far too complex for them to unravel, without their first processing the fundamental knowledge of what it is they are seeking.

Even in the world of science, which is a closer approximation of the physical world, it is acknowledged that there are no absolutes. If science were to accept absolutes, the field of scientific inquiry would come to an end.

There are those who are in search of the truth. This is an endless search that will take one nowhere. If we ever find out exactly who we are, it will be the end of the human intellect. Whether they realize it or not, most people continue to undergo change in their values, outlook and understanding. This process has no finality. Human beings are constantly evolving organisms. The question that remains is: how does one select, of the very many alternatives, that which is relevant?

A brief course in preliminary scientific principles enables a person to better understand the world they live in and their relationship to it. We can only view the world with our receptors and the degree of linguistic precision that we acquire in our culture. No human being can view anything with the certain knowledge that they are perceiving it as it really is. For instance, if a mouse could write it would describe the dog as an enormous creature; whereas the giraffe would take issue with that and say it is a tiny creature from his elevated point of view. They are both telling the "truth" as they see it but only from their limited point of view.

Other questions are asked such as "What is the meaning of life?" "What is consciousness and the mysteries of the mind?" "Why am I here?" "What is my relationship to God and the universe?" These same questions have been asked over the centuries, and most are totally irrelevant to achieving social progress and, eventually parity. These are examples of unanswerable questions because none have a valid point of reference. Does the posing of such ambiguous questions express concern over the condition of one's fellow human beings, or a desire to elevate their condition? Of course not. Such musings are pure gibberish, as impotent as wailing over an injured person rather than seeking medical attention.

Take, for example, the question "what is life, its meaning and our relationship to the universe?" an ultimately hollow and meaningless question. There is no effort put out by these philosophers, poets and metaphysicians for the genuine pursuit of the processes in question. They understand so little about the mechanisms of the physical processes of nature, yet those asking such questions don't go into the lab in pursuit of this process or try to understand even the structure of a single cell, let alone the universe. They are merely repeating the quotations other verbalists have made for centuries, while making no effort to verify the validity of their assumptions. Although they feel these questions are profound, in this context, they are actually naive.

Besides, with such questions about the process we call life we make an assumption that life has "meaning." Actually, as difficult as it may for some to accept, the only meaning it has is that which we give it. Genuine concern for understanding such profound questions is manifested by engaging in a research program where examine the characteristics and mechanics of living systems. This is precisely the same analytic principle by which an increase in criminal behavior requires an investigation into the nature and factors that shape human behavior.

Merely talking about the things that we do not understand does not add to our knowledge. For example the word "instinct" does not tell us anything more about the behavior of the organism involved. It is a word assigned to patterns of behavior many do not understand. Instead of the word instinct, we need precise information on the actual processes behind such things as how fish migrate, how birds build nests, and how organisms undergo adaptation.

One may reasonably ask: Why do people cling to the values of the past, when they seem so obviously irrelevant to the present? Part of this, of course, is that long-standing thought patterns are often hard to overcome — particularly when they appear to serve the interests of the individual. The old way of thinking is simpler and easier to handle. In a two-valued way of thinking, such as good and bad, right and wrong, love and hate, cause and effect, very little analytic process is involved.

Also, many of us are ill equipped in analytical thinking. Analytical thinking requires an understanding of process relationships and a broad range of information. We are insufficiently equipped and trained to objectively evaluate alternative proposals. Science today is taught as if it were a series of discrete specialties, as if biology and chemistry and physics ere not really a single science. No school we know of presents science in a holistic and significant way. Students learn narrow principles and laws and processes, rather than the scientific way of thinking. This makes it very difficult for the average person to apply scientific and analytical thinking in their everyday lives.

That is the main reason ignorance prevails. People want answers instantly, ones they can easily grasp and use immediately — even ones with no basis in fact. Science does not provide quick ultimate answers. It merely presents information about the physical world we live in. The scientific community recommends a system to best explain how it is that nature functions the way it does.

The challenge scientists must confront in the near future is to develop methods of presenting science and technology in a language easily assimilated by those less familiar with the scientific method. This may be accomplished through films, books, videos and CD's, to help bridge the difference between science and irrelevance. At present most of these difficulties lie in the field of communication and education. We recommend *The Demon-Haunted world: Science as a Candle in The Dark*, by Carl Sagan to anyone interested in exploring this area.

The reason we emphasize science is that science-oriented individuals present their findings without any regard as to whether people like it. Often at the risk of their social standing, careers, or even their lives, they hold fast to such concepts as the earth being neither flat nor the center of the universe, the theory of evolution, and the fact that illness is not due to punishment by gods or demons. This differs vastly from politicians who seek public approbation by catering to the dominant values of the times. We see examples of this in such emotional populist issues as family values, nationalism, and religion.

Most churches make people feel guilty about natural human inclinations, making them dependent on the church for forgiveness. While religion caters to unresolved human problems such as insecurity, shame, fear, wish fulfillment, and offers hope for a better life if not in this world then the next, science offers people the tools of reason and knowledge to help build self-reliance and free people from the mythology of wish fulfillment.

All human beings have the potential to develop their own concepts, and to make their own — heaven or hell here on earth. But there is no way for these refugees from reality to perceive the actual state of affairs without putting out tremendous effort and inquiry to translate their wishes and dreams into a working reality. It takes this honest effort to understand the nature of the world we live in.

Should people turn to science for answers, most are not sophisticated enough to state the problems correctly, let alone grasp the response to their inquiries. Following the path of least resistance in our thinking, however, only holds us back from making a more appropriate evaluation of any area of our investigation. This makes it easier to understand how dictators such as Hitler succeed in building a large following, particularly during hard times.

In seeking simplified answers they blame many social problems on minorities, foreigners, karma, auras that are believed to surround each individual, acts of demons or gods, or the position of the planets at the time of one's birth, just to name a few. Others seek to bring out higher levels of human consciousness and self-realization through meditation. To the uninformed these are easy to understand, because they do not demand concrete proof or verifiable evidence. Hence the popularity of metaphysics. Some insist that insist we return to the simpler life of the past, to the "good old days." This is another myth that some people cling to, that things were somehow "better" in times of less technological development.

This is unfortunately a growing phenomenon in the scientifically illiterate world. Even some scientists today are persuaded by pseudo-science. In a sense, even scientists are victims of culture. The proof of this lies in the fact that some have been persuaded to use their abilities to make weapons of destruction with little thought to the consequences of their actions.

The belief, also, that science or religion would not conform to the indoctrination of totalitarianism is a continuing myth. At various times in recent history, in countries such as Spain, Italy, Russia, Japan and Germany, areas of science gave way to sadism and even the practitioners of one of the most ethical professions — medicine — performed gruesome experiments on living people. Many churches of nations at war could be found blessing tanks, soldiers and battleships ships, even when the combatants on both sides were members of the same denomination.

There is really no such thing as a pure scientist, as all data is interpreted on the basis of personal background and experience. Some people may be said to be scientific in their specialized discipline while in other areas of physical science they may be illiterate. Actually formulating conclusions outside of one's particular discipline would be a violation of the scientific method.

Science should not be used for the conquest of nature, but rather to point out our interdependence and connectivity to nature, and to explore how to utilize our knowledge to live in accordance with the natural order of things. When we as a nation spend nearly three hundred billion dollars annually on defense and only two billion towards understanding our environment, one must question whether there is actually intelligent life on Earth.

The only hope for the development of a new civilization for humankind is to accept the responsibility for improving our lives through knowledge, understanding and a deeper comprehension of humanity's relationship to natural processes of evolution. Our future is determined by the effort that we put forth to achieve this transition.

Furthermore, when we finally outgrow assumptions of superior and inferior races and realize the unity of humankind and its true relationship with the planet, we will achieve the full potentials of science for humane development. This could serve as a unifying, global force for the achievement of a sustainable world.

But not knowing where we are, how can we possibly know where we are headed?

CHAPTER 5

NEW FRONTIERS OF SOCIAL CHANGE

IN OUR DYNAMIC UNIVERSE ALL THINGS CHANGE, from the state of the farthest reaches of outer space to the movement of the continents. The same process of change occurs in all living and nonliving systems. The history of civilization is the story of change from the simple to the more complex. Human ingenuity and invention bear witness to this fact. No system can remain static for long. Unfortunately, the changes are not always for the best.

Although we accept the inevitability of change, humans meet change with considerable resistance. Those in charge, whether of a religious, military, socialist, capitalist, communist, or tribal institution or society, will attempt to hold back change, because change threatens those in control. Even those oppressed by a social system may support it and the status quo because it is familiar and known. No matter how oppressive one's surroundings, there is comfort in the familiar.

Human civilization is no exception to this process of change. Change occurs to all social systems, and is the only constant. The history of humankind is one of change, which is either brought about by natural circumstance or by the direct intervention of human effort.

Technology influences the most remote regions of the world almost as fast as the technology develops. In 1993 Malaysia had interests in banking, construction, issuing of credit cards, fast food outlets, manufacturing of medical supplies, and information technologies.

Untouched, isolated cultures are fast becoming the stuff of history. Although many native peoples still wear ancestral dress, they also carry video cameras and other state-of-the-art electronic devices. These invasions of newer technologies are present from Papua New Guinea to Vietnam to China. In Thailand, we find Siam Cement, one of the largest cement companies in the world. Some of the most successful cement companies in the world can also be found in Colombia and Peru. In our own country, Disney Information has replaced US Steel in digitally transmitted information.

Yet at every turn, vested interests oppose technological change. Earlier this century defenders of the horse-mounted cavalry delayed development of the tank; so entrenched was this tradition that when Germany invaded Poland in 1939, their Panzers faced Polish soldiers still mounted on horseback.

It was immediately and fatally obvious that the tank had rendered the horse soldiers obsolete. Later the development of aircraft threatened the tank divisions. Pilots and aircraft designers fought to hold back the development of guided missiles. The missile men fought to hold back the development of laser weapons.

In a similar manner the established social order tends to perpetuate itself. Those in positions of power are able and highly motivated to delay conditions that would advance society as a whole.

From the introduction of agriculture some 10,000 years ago until recent history — specifically, the advent of the Machine Age in the late seventeenth and early eighteenth centuries — the rate of this change was slow. Social change in times past crept along, accompanied by a great deal of human suffering during the transition from one phase of civilization to another. Since the Industrial Revolution, change continues to accelerate at a fantastic rate. In technologically advanced cultures, change occurs rapidly — often too rapidly for the average person to comprehend or adjust to. And even when individual adjust, our institutions of — government, education, medicine and industrial cannot. Their size, their infrastructure, their very processes and missions resist and oppose rapid change.

In just a few decades the transfer of information moved from the telegraph to radio to television to wireless transmission computers to satellites that can store trillions of bits of data and transmit this to any part of the globe instantaneously.

Many of us forget or are not aware of the fact that less than forty years ago it took a pair of wires to carry a dozen conversations. Twenty years later, one cable conveyed thirty thousand conversations simultaneously. Today a single laser beam carries more than a million. This explosion of technology can no longer be stopped.

Whether the citizenry of the world is capable of grasping the significance of such prodigious changes is actually irrelevant. What is required and really significant is that a sufficient number of the world's leaders be able to comprehend developments of this magnitude. The degree to which we are able to comprehend such developments will determine our chances of survival.

Technological changes occur less rapidly in lesser-developed countries. Many of the systems and methodologies of some nations have been remained for hundreds, even thousands, of years. Small groups of people, such as the headhunters of the Amazon, still live in places where their social and physical environment remains relatively static. They can still be found making the same kinds of rafts and other tools, and utilizing the same techniques as their ancestors did a thousand years ago.

Stagnation is not confined to the underdeveloped countries; even today among developed countries there are large national groups of people who cling tenaciously to the past as the benefits of civilization pass them by. But the future is no respecter of the dominant values of today. And the generations to come will evolve a set of values unique to that phase of civilization.

While behavior patterns may have remained unchanged for thousands of years in these low-technology societies, the notion that people may be carbon copies of their predecessors is untrue in today's technological world. New generations immersed in different environments require different solutions.

With the advent of the World Wide Web, cybernation and artificial intelligence, the rate of change is being greatly accelerated. Possibly in the next ten years we will see more changes than those wrought by the past events of recorded history. If we as a nation fail to adapt to these changes others will pass us by. The future belongs to those capable of meeting these challenges.

To be sure, technology evolves at its own rate; one thing triggers another, leading to wider applications. Future technologies evolve at their own pace, determined by many interrelated factors. If we attempt to alter our social evolution faster than the ability of society to adapt to change, there will be severe consequences. Rapid changes without the proper preparations generate severe problems. The development of social systems unresponsive to people and their environment only increases our internal strife.

Common crises create common bonds. While people seek advantage during the good times, shared suffering draws people together. We have seen this behavior repeated time and time again throughout the centuries, during times of flood, famine, fire, or natural disasters. When the threat passes, people return to seeking advantage over others.

Motion pictures like *Independence Day* depict a world united to repel an invasion by a superior, hostile alien culture. Indeed, it seems that the only force that would mobilize the world in a unified direction would be one that poses a common threat, such as a huge meteor heading towards the earth or some other major catastrophe. In such an event, border disputes would cease and become irrelevant to the impending disaster. While many would call upon their deities to intervene, nations would unite and call upon science and technology to help solve a common threat. Bankers and lawyers, businessmen and politicians would be bypassed. *All of the resources for total mobilization would be harnessed without any concern for monetary cost or profit.* Under this kind of threatening condition, most people realize where their survival lies.

As global challenges and scientific information proliferate, we face common threats that transcend national boundaries: overpopulation, energy shortages, environmental pollution, water scarcity, economic catastrophe, the spread of uncontrollable diseases and the technological displacement of people by machines threaten us all. Although many people are dedicated to alleviating these problems, our social and environmental problems will remain insurmountable as long as a few powerful nations and financial interests maintain control of and consume most of the world's resources.

Although people, publications, and multi-media presentations paint spectacular pictures of the developments to come in such areas as transportation, housing, and medicine, they ignore the fact that, in a monetary-based economy, the full benefits of these developments continue to be distributed to a relative few. What is not touched upon is how the new technologies of the future can be used to organize societies and economies efficiently and equitably so that everyone may benefit from them.

Currently, no think tanks conduct brainstorming sessions how to align social organization with the advancements of technology. No government or industrial group plans for the displacement of people by machines.

Many people believe that in the event of social breakdown the government will ensure their survival. This is highly improbable. In the event of such a breakdown, the existing government would most likely declare a state of emergency in an attempt to prevent total chaos. A review of actions taken by governments facing social collapse over the last few decades shows that their primary concern is preserving existing institutions and power structures — even though these may be a chief contributing factor to the problem.

Many people throughout history have taken politicians to task for actions that have not been on the people's behalf. The reasons for this may become clearer when one accepts the fact that even in modern democracies, these leaders are not elected to improve the life of the average person: rather, they are appointed to maintain the preferential positions of many of the established order.

There are growing indications of awareness on the part of people in various areas of the world that events have gone beyond the control of political leaders. Everywhere we can see political figures and parties come and go, political strategies adopted and discarded for their inability to satisfy the demands of one faction or another.

The reason we do not stress writing your congressman, or any number of governmental agencies, is that they lack the necessary knowledge to deal with our problems. Their focus is on preserving existing systems, not on changing them. It appears there are few within the present day societies who want to phase themselves out. In modern industrial societies the cause of inaction lies within the cumbersome political process itself, an anachronism in an era when most decisions can be made on any important issue in a split second by the objective entry of data into computers.

Real social change occurs when conditions deteriorate to such an extent that governments, politicians, and social institutions no longer have the support and confidence of the people. What once worked is acknowledged as no longer relevant or acceptable. When the public is better informed or in sufficient pain, only then is it possible to introduce a new social arrangement.

Unfortunately, the majority of people today respond to simplistic answers, which tends to repeat the cycle of events. When faced with intolerable social conditions, many of the older patterns will emerge again as people attempt to find someone or something to blame for the conditions (blacks, Jews, or homosexuals, for instance) or as they seek refuge in religion or a belief in supernatural forces.

Significant social changes are not brought about by men and women of reason and good will on a personal level. The notion that one can sit and talk to individuals and alter their values is highly improbable. If the person one is talking to does not have the fundamental knowledge of the operation of scientific principles and the processes of natural laws, it is difficult for them to understand how things fit together on a holistic level.

The solutions to our problems will not come about through the application of reason or logic. We do not live in a reasonable or logical world. There is no historical record of any society that deliberately and consciously modified their culture to fit changing times. The real factors responsible for social change result from biosocial pressures inherent in all social systems. It is brought about by natural or economic occurrences which immediately threaten large numbers of people.

Some of these conditions responsible for social change include limited resources, war, overpopulation, epidemics, natural disasters, economic recession, downsizing on a mass scale, technological displacement of people by machines and the failure of their appointed leaders to overcome these problems.

Change can come from disasters or from major technological advances. The introduction of agriculture brought about a significant change in society, as did the Industrial Revolution and the introduction of the medium of money to the exchange process. From an historical perspective all of these appear positive. At the time of their inception, however, people lost their jobs, new skills were required, whole ways of life disappeared.

The direction change takes is not always for the better or for the improvement of the human condition. Change is risky when scarcity, artificial or real, drives the economy and power-seeking leaders command weapons powerful enough to annihilate entire populations and render our planet uninhabitable. Humankind's potential for creativity and innovation far exceeds its inclination to destroy — yet every time that we exercise destructive power, we take a thousands steps backward for every few forward.

Certainly, not all change has been beneficial to humanity or to the integrity of the planet's life support systems. For this reason, many people desire a return to earlier and simpler times. But it has been demonstrated that any effective, large-scale and permanent social transformation cannot be achieved through the development of small, cooperative and hand-tooled economies. These cooperative ventures have been tried throughout history by both religious and secular interests. Most failed to achieve or sustain their desired goals. The reason for the failure was not due to human nature or greed. The primary cause of their demise was the fact that most participants, although sincere, had little information on the primary factors responsible for human behavior.

Although individuals throughout history have proposed many ideal social arrangements — from Plato's Republic through the modern Utopians — no industrial nation have ever proposed an arrangement to improve the lives of all people and build a truly civilized nation. This is not difficult to understand when one considers the overall principles that govern the social system. The government's principles are based on ownership and the accumulation of wealth, power and property.

Visionaries of sincere intent write and speak eloquently of a world moving forward in unity and brotherhood. Many expect a worldwide epiphany or transformational event. Others expect reason to prevail. Only a very few propose plans to achieve unity, some of which appear incomplete and pose a threat to existing institutions and to national and self-interest: the architects of such plans are often classified as agitators, impractical utopians, and disrupters.

A few bold attempts to achieve world unification failed because movement leaders had no real understanding of the primary forces that shape social evolution. Most significantly, they sought their solutions within the framework of the monetary system, never realizing that physical resources — not money — are the real necessity where the ability of any social system to sustain its people is concerned.

Although the monetary system served to help to eliminate the old, cumbersome rates of exchange in a barter system, it is by no means the final answer. The history of civilization indicates continuing evolution and adaptation. No single answer is able to serve all time, all peoples, and all problems.

Our outmoded social, political, and international order is no longer appropriate to these times. Our outworn social institutions cannot grasp or adapt to the ability of innovative technology to achieve good, nor can they overcome the inequities forced upon so many.

Competition and scarcity have instilled an atmosphere of jealousy and mistrust within people and nations. The concepts of proprietary rights, manifested in the corporate entity and in the sovereignty of nations, inhibit the free exchange of information that is necessary to meet global challenges.

Many people fee the pain of change and yearn to return to a simpler time of "traditional" values. Their vision is faulty. Those times were not, in fact, so good. In the first fifty years of that "simpler" time, we waged two world wars. In the intervening years a major agricultural and economic disaster sent millions to soup kitchens and breadlines. If they are honest, it is not the fantasy of the "good old days" that they wish to see realized, but more simplicity that they want.

Our problems today are enormous and global in their scope and impact. They cannot be solved by any one nation. The concept of common good is global in nature, local in implementation. We cannot hope to backtrack to traditional values, which no longer apply. Any attempt to retreat into the methods of the past would condemn untold millions to a life of needless misery, toil, and suffering.

I am not advocating that these older institutions be overthrown: it is just that they are becoming unworkable. Unfortunately, it will most likely take a social and economic breakdown to bring about the demise of the old system and its institutions. At this point the only significant social change will probably occur when a sufficient amount of people, through economic failure, lose confidence in their elected officials. The public will then demand other alternatives. While we would like to think that this could usher in a bright new chapter in the human drama, it is far more likely that the most probable course will be a form of dictatorship, perhaps even an American brand of fascism, ostensibly presented to the people as a way of protecting them from the products of their own inadequate culture.

However, it is not enough to point out the limiting factors that may threaten the survivability of all nations. The challenge all cultures now face in this technological age — some more than others — is to provide a smooth transition towards the introduction of a new way of thinking about ourselves, the environment and the management of human affairs.

It is now mandatory that all nations engage in a joint venture, planning on a global scale for new alternatives with a relevant orientation toward social arrangements. This is the only option if we are to avoid the unavoidable decline of the civilized world. If humankind is to come together toward a mutual prosperity, universal access to resources is essential.

Along with a new orientation toward human and environmental concerns, there must be the *methodology for making this a reality*. If these ends are to be achieved, the monetary system must eventually be surpassed by a world **resource-based economy**. To effectively and economically utilize resources, the necessary cybernated and computerized technology must be applied to ensure a higher standard of living for everyone. With the intelligent and humane application of science and technology, we will be able to guide and shape our future for the preservation of the environment, ourselves and for generations to come.

It is not enough to advocate the cooperation of all nations. We need a global society based upon a practical blueprint acceptable to the world's people. We also need an international planning council capable of translating the blueprint and the advantages that would be gained by world unification.

The design must be based upon the carrying capacity of our planet, its resources and the needs of its inhabitants. To sustain our civilization, we must coordinate advanced technology and available resources within a humane systems approach.

Many of the professions familiar to us today will eventually be phased out. With the rate of change now taking place, a vast array of occupations will become obsolete and disappear. In a society that applies a systems approach, these professions will be replaced by interdisciplinary teams — the systems analysts, computer programmers, operation researchers, and those who link the world together in vast communications networks.

We have the skills and the knowledge to apply interdisciplinary teams to problems. However, only in times of war or national emergencies do we call upon and assemble interdisciplinary teams to help find workable solutions to social problems. If we mobilize the same resources for our social problems as we do during a war, beneficial effects on a large scale can be achieved in a relatively short time. This could easily be accomplished by utilizing many of our universities' training facilities and staffs to best determine possible alternative methods to solve these problems.

This approach would be an important initial phase to define the possible parameters for the future of all civilization.

The process of social change must allow for changing conditions that continuously update the design parameters, and for the infusion of new technologies into emerging cultures. Design teams utilizing socially integrated computers can automatically be informed of any changes in conditions.

In this world of constant change it is no longer a question of whether we choose to make the necessary changes. Our very survival demands that we act on this challenge and adopt these new requirements.

CHAPTER 6

THE INHUMANITY OF A MONETARY-BASED SYSTEM

ALTHOUGH SKILLFUL ADVERTISERS LEAD US TO BELIEVE otherwise, in today's monetary-based economies, the human consequences of introducing new technologies seldom concern those introducing the technology. In a monetary-based system, the major aim of industry is profit: maintaining the competitive edge and the bottom line appears to be all that matters. The social and health problems that arise from mass unemployment of people, often of workers who are rendered obsolete by the infusion of automation, are considered irrelevant, if they are considered at all.

Any social need that may be met is secondary to acquiring a profit for the business. If the profit is insufficient, the service will be withdrawn. Everything is subordinate to increasing the profit margin for shareholders. It does not serve the interest of a monetary-based society to engage in the production of goods and services to enhance the lives of people as a goal — no more than manmade laws are enacted to protect the lives of its citizens.

All of the world's economic systems — socialism, communism, fascism, and even our free enterprise capitalist system — perpetuate social stratification, elitism, nationalism and racism, primarily based on economic disparity. As long as a social system uses money or barter, people and nations will seek differential advantage by maintaining the economic competitive edge or, if they cannot do so by means of commerce, by military intervention.

War represents the supreme failure of nations to resolve their differences. From a strictly pragmatic standpoint, it is the most inefficient waste of lives and resources ever conceived. This crude and violent attempt to resolve international differences takes on even more ominous overtones with the advent of elaborate computerized thermonuclear delivery systems, deadly diseases and chemicals, and the threat of sabotage to a nation's computer networks. Even when nations desire peace, they usually lack the knowledge to arrive at peaceful solutions.

War is not the only form of violence imposed on the populace by inadequate social arrangements. There is also hunger, poverty, and scarcity. The use of money and the creation of debt foster economic insecurity, a condition that perpetuates crime, lawlessness, and resentment. Paper proclamations and treaties do not alter the facts of scarcity and insecurity, while nationalism tends only to help propagate the separation of nations and the world's people.

Even a peace treaty cannot prevent another war if the underlying causes are not addressed. The unworkable aspects of international law tend to freeze things as they are. Nations that have conquered land all over the world by force and violence would still retain their positions of territorial and resource advantage, regardless of treaties. Such agreements serve only as temporary suspensions to conflict.

But focusing our efforts on non-productive and non-creative endeavors wastes lives as surely as war does. Throughout history we have lived through ages characterized by wasted lives, in which the abilities of a great many people have not been fully realized of utilized. Countless time, efforts, and minds are wasted in the pursuit of money and on occupations that contribute nothing to the human intellect or condition.

From the earliest civilizations to the present day, most humans have had to work to earn a living. Our attitudes about work may be a carryover from earlier times.

During the thousands of years of the monetary system, most workers have been paid just enough to make it necessary that they return to work — even when higher wages have been possible. How else can the wage-payer keep the workers coming back? If the employee received wages that allowed them to work a few weeks and then take time off for a world cruise, an extended vacation, or other such luxuries, production schedules would suffer. Even the highly educated and affluent who live in more expensive homes and drive expensive cars have to appear at a place of work if they wish to maintain their standard of living. All of us — even the very top executives — are indentured slaves of the monetary system. Most of us suffer from the fact that we lack a meaningful existence. We stay at jobs we hate to buy more gadgets we don't need, or to build up earned time off so we can escape from the reason we need a vacation in the first place.

In the workaday world many of us are frantically busy trying to stay afloat, making payments on cars, homes, and material possessions that enslave the body and mind in an endless attempt to secure our future. Although many today take home much more money, the value of the dollar through inflation has decreased the purchasing power for most people. We are caught up in the game of getting ahead, without even thinking about what or whom we're trying to get ahead of. Most of us do not take the time to think about our own lives and how we relate to one another, or to what and who we really are.

Even those who achieve economic security have become addicted to the media's image of personal success. When we achieve our first economic goal, we want more— the cabin cruiser, the vacation house, and the trip abroad. In this monetary world even our dreams are rationed. We start out with "If only I can make a decent living". If we achieve that, we progress to "If only we had the little house in the country to get away to, then we'd be happy." At each successive gain in this endless chain of dissatisfaction we acquire more and more material wealth, but it's never enough to make us happy. We live in a world of unfulfilled dreams in which we never really come to know or understand what constitutes a meaningful life.

In the future people may view our present phase of civilization as an age of intellectual and economic insufficiency. They may find it difficult to understand how we could have accepted aggression and competition as being normal. Some mothers and fathers have even made attempts to secure the future for their daughters and sons by having them marry into a secure position of wealth. This is an accepted form of prostitution or selling to the highest bidder.

In a monetary system even democracy is an illusion perpetuated to give the populace a feeling of participation in a so-called democratic process. In most instances people nominated for public representation are pre-selected by the power elite and serve the interests of the highest bidder. Political parties are a perfect example: a single party representative runs against another party's single representative. The fantasy is that whichever one wins immediately represents everyone in the election area — regardless of political party or philosophy.

The country's actions and most of the decisions are made by and for the major corporations, financial interests, the most wealthy, and the military industrial complex. As long as money and a monetary system prevail, true democracy will continue to be nothing much more than an illusion.

We must stop constantly fighting to attain human rights and equal justice in an unjust system, and start building a society where equal rights are an *integral part of the design.*

As long as we remain in a monetary system, most people will never have the money to behave democratically. A person may desire a particular type of house and car, but might lack the means to purchase it. How has this person benefited from the democratic process or the freedom to choose? Yet we claim to have a democratic system that is the best form of government in the world. In actuality we are really only as free as our purchasing power enables us to be. And with money so concentrated in the hands of so few, even this freedom is illusory.

Despite its title and treatment by the media the Federal Reserve System that issues and controls our currency *is not* an agency of the federal government run for the benefit of people. Rather the "Fed" is a private institution run solely by and for private profit and even the amount in reserve is questionable.

The Federal Reserve, a private institution deceptively named, has enormous influence over our government, its leaders, our personal savings accounts, and to a large extent over how many of us will have jobs. The Federal Reserve, not the government, has complete control over the lending of money. This means it sets interest rates for our country, thereby maintaining tremendous political influence.

But the Federal Reserve System is not the only private institution that manipulates our economic system. Banks use a process called "fractional reserve banking" that enables them to loan much more money than they have assets on deposit, to cover the loans. They then charge interest on money they don't have. Through this process banks lend out at least ten times more money than they have on reserve, which reduces the value of our money and leads to inflation. It is no wonder the newest and biggest buildings in all cities belong to banks. Of course, if we behave as the banks do we would be charged with fraud.

This is not a new practice. In 1881, James Garfield stated "Whoever controls the volume of money in any country is absolute master of all industry and commerce. And when you realize that the entire system is very easily controlled one way or another by a few powerful men at the top, you will not have to be told how periods of inflation and depression originate."

Private money lenders understood early on the overwhelming benefits of lending money to nations at war when the paybacks were assured by the taxation of their people. This was much more profitable than lending to individuals Financial interests and corporations instigate wars and disruptions to this very day.

Furthermore, the monetary system avoids the crises of the lack of purchasing power of individuals and small companies by propping up the economy through military expenditures, corporate welfare and providing funds for research to private industries. The government borrows money from private lending institutions to help support the economy in these areas. This increases the national debt while directing the public's attention away from national problems such as cutting expenditures from the veterans administration, aid to the poor, education, environmental concerns, etc. In many instances our government and corporations use our own military equipment and the use of force to put down revolutionary social changes elsewhere in the world, while generating an illusion of prosperity at home.

Amschel Rothschild, one of the early beneficiaries of the private banking system, stated, *"Give me the power to issue and control a nation's money and I care not who makes its laws."* *As it is applied today, financial power is truly amoral.*

A truly democratic system works only when all people have access to the same opportunities for individual development and economic growth. This requirement is not the goal of a monetary-based system.

In a free enterprise system, people who design and build a ski resort don't submit the design to a democratic vote in which all participate. Instead they submit it to the demands of the market, that is, those who can afford to ski. If they offer enough of the amenities that skiers want and can afford, their resort succeeds. A successful system should cater to the needs of all people. There are many people who would like to ski who can't afford to participate. Again, the choices are limited to what a certain group of people can afford. *This is elitism.*

Wherever money is involved, there is always a kind of elitism. Those who control the purchasing power always have a far greater influence.

Many years ago the American people were first taxed to build roads for automobiles. They did not vote for this development. The automobile and bus industries, real estate lobbies and military greatly influenced the development of freeways and roads because of the potential for automobiles and land sales represented by the expansion of the highway system. Many cities offered transportation systems that were far cleaner, more efficient, and more economical than automobiles, but these were sold out and dismantled by the influence of the vested interests representing the automobile industry.

As a result, we have a transportation system that has resulted in urban sprawl, the loss of millions of acres of natural areas and croplands, air and water pollution, thousands of people killed or injured each year and transportation that is so expensive that a great number of Americans cannot afford to participate. For what and for whom has democracy worked in this case? Millions of Americans taxed for highways in which they do not share in the benefits and which have proved dangerous, inefficient and expensive as a means of transportation?

In our present monetary system private institutions hoard a great deal of useful knowledge, rather than making it readily available to the entire world's people. In an increasingly proprietary and commercial world, in which even college professors talk of copyrighting the notes from their lectures, there is a disturbing shift from the spirit of the pioneer to that of the salesman.

Several companies recently submitted and received patents on the genome of two men immune to AIDS. The companies neither created nor own the genetic material — nor did they discover them independent of the living bearers of those genes. But they acquired patents on genes in living humans. Is this democracy in action? At this writing, at least one of the men has threatened legal action. Rather than meeting the challenges of elevating the human condition, the scientist increasingly morphs into the businessman, auctioning the benefits of his or her efforts to the highest bidder. For this reason, a great deal of new technology still remains in the control of private institutions rather than the public domain.

Many of our heroes in the past have been honored for their self-sacrifice in attempting to make the world a better place. Thousands have sacrificed their lives; others have been tortured and imprisoned during their attempts to better the lives of others. Very often these people acted as they did without thought for monetary rewards.

The big lie that has been perpetuated by those in control of the money system is that only competition generates incentive. This system may be said to provide employment and incentive, but it also produces greed, corruption, crime, embezzlement etc. For centuries, all governments have directly and indirectly programmed their subjects with a value system that perpetuates the control group. They have successfully used the human mind as a dumping ground to store their own values and concepts along with behavioral patterns that generate feelings of guilt at any departure from the dominant values of the established system.

At the same time, these control groups have stifled the development of individuality by fostering compliant populations which lack both the information and the insight to pose the question, "Where, exactly, so my values come from?"

The monetary system places a tremendous, unnecessary strain on available resources, and denies access to the benefits of mass production to countless millions of people. In a monetary-based society profit depends on maintaining an artificial scarcity of goods and services or on the conscious withdrawal of efficiency.

Rather than designing automotive styles to last for many years, manufacturers waste tremendous amounts of energy in retooling for yearly changes to compete for market share with others producing machines that serve exactly the same function. A recent military survey of commercial catalogs identified over 300 types of wrenches, differing so slightly that many were interchangeable. While a wrench is a useful tool, what purpose is served by over 300 minimal-varying models? Tremendous waste in materials and resources result from each company doing unnecessary and redundant paper work, advertising, manufacturing, etc.

A further example can be seen whenever a famous figure addresses the nation on television. The viewer will see dozens of different microphones, each representing a competing media-group. Actually only one or two are necessary to report the event throughout the world.

And consider the fashion industry, where clothing has to constantly change in order to induce people to purchase the newest, latest fads.

In the United States during periods of "price wars" milk and other agricultural products were destroyed to maintain higher price levels. Where is our outrage? We buy into the old "virtue" of work while we allow its essential products to be destroyed. Equally damaging, however, is planned obsolescence, where industries deliberately create products that break and require replacement or unnecessary repairs.

In the aircraft industry, sales of large transport aircraft are not the major source of profit. Large profits come from the maintenance and replacement of parts. This is particularly so within the military, with its dependence on the market. Vendor changes affect sustainment costs far more than changes in mission. Even during World War II, many anti-aircraft guns and armaments were manufactured from parts that were not interchangeable. The parts from one company would not fit the guns of another company.

Today Congress pushes the Defense Department to "save money" by purchasing commercial-off-the-shelf equipment. On the surface, buying already available equipment, rather than developing military-specific equipment, appears sensible. However, military equipment must be interoperable as well as supportable all over the world — and in environments that commercial equipment seldom encounters. Personal computers sent with troops to Desert storm, for example, failed by the hundreds in the excessive heat and sand encountered in Kuwait. And, instead of buying parts for a single model, the military now must accommodate multiple vendors and their equipment, parts and tools. Our tax money flows far outside government channels. This should surprise no one. Even a cursory review of the annual defense budget finds numerous examples of Congressionally-mandated purchases of equipment and services that are of no use to the military. So in addition to personally buying goods that keep companies in business, your taxes also go to them.

Over a half century ago the United States Electric Light Company gave its dynamic inventor Hiram Maxim a twenty thousand-dollar annual life pension and exiled him to

England. They needed to get rid of him because he kept inventing improvements. His creative ability made their equipment obsolete before they had the time to pay for it.

Unfortunately for the people in the U.S., Maxim produced some of his greatest inventions in England. At the same time he was being knighted for his outstanding accomplishments, the United States Electric Light Company was going out of business. In Japan today the shelf life of electronic equipment before obsolescence is approximately 3 months.

A money system has existed for centuries and, whether we realize it or not, has always been used to control the behavior of those with limited purchasing power. Money has no influence where resources and access are not limited. It is only when resources are scarce that a monetary or barter system can function.

In other words, if a person wants to obtain goods and services he or she is obligated to submit to the control of others. For example, when a person goes to work in any industry today, they enter a private dictatorship from the moment they punch the time clock to the time they leave the premises.

We are long past due for a serious examination and radical overhaul of our economic system and ideologies. Attempting to find solutions to the monumental problems within our present society will only serve as temporary patchwork, prolonging an obsolete system. Our competitive monetary system alone did not give us a high standard of living in the United States. Our advantages also come from being isolated from hostile, neighboring countries, from our wide range of natural resources, our fertile land and the many contributions of inventors and engineers, and from our production technology.

CHAPTER 7

WHEN MONEY
BECOMES IRRELEVANT

IN THIS CHAPTER WE WILL DISCUSS a straightforward approach to the redesign of a culture, in which the age-old inadequacies of war, poverty, hunger, debt, and unnecessary human suffering are viewed not only as avoidable, but totally unacceptable. This new social design works towards eliminating the underlying causes that are responsible for many of our problems, but they cannot be eliminated within the framework of the present monetary and political establishment.

The major corporations' first concern is profit. This narrow vision will ultimately result in the demise of our economic system. If the monetary system continues to operate, we face ever-increasing technological unemployment, today referred to as downsizing. We need fewer people with greater skills to support our production. Everyone else becomes irrelevant — except as consumers of that production. It is only a matter of time until automation replaces people in almost all areas, resulting in the lack of purchasing power for people to buy the goods turned out. Even with an expanding market, such a situation will inevitably bring about massive and unmanageable problems.

During the 1930's, at the height of the Great Depression, the Roosevelt administration enacted new social legislation designed to minimize revolutionary tendencies and to address the problems of unemployment by providing jobs through the WPA, CC Camps, NRA, transient camps, and the federal arts projects. Ultimately, however, it was World War II that pulled the U.S. out of that worldwide recession. If we permit current conditions to take their natural course, we will soon be faced with another international recession of even greater magnitude.

Although at the beginning of World War II, the US had only 600 first class fighting aircraft, we rapidly increased production to 90,000 planes per year. Did we have enough money to pay for the required implements of war? No, there was not enough money or gold, but we did have more than enough resources. Available resources and personnel — not funding — provided production and efficiency required to win the war.

We live in a culture that seems to work collectively only in response to a crisis. Only in times of war or national disaster do we move beyond money and apply the necessary resources and assemble interdisciplinary teams to meet a threat. Rarely, if ever, do we employ such concerted efforts to find workable solutions to social problems.

If we applied the same efforts of scientific mobilization toward social betterment as we do during a war or disaster, large-scale results could be achieved in a relatively short time. Much more time and effort must be directed toward the collection of experimental evidence to support innovative social arrangements.

The Earth is abundant with resources; today our practice of rationing resources through monetary methods is irrelevant and counterproductive to the well-being of people. Modern society has access to highly advanced technologies and can easily provide more than enough for a very high standard of living for all the earth's people by implementing a **resource-based economy.**

Simply stated, a resource-based economy utilizes existing resources rather than money, and provides an equitable method of distribution in the most humane and efficient manner for the entire population. It is a system in which all natural, man-made, machine-made, and synthetic resources are available without the use of money, credits, barter, or any other form of debt. A resource-based economy utilizes existing resources from the land and sea, physical equipment, industrial plants, etc. to enhance the lives of the total population. In an economy based on resources rather than money, we can easily produce all of the necessities of life and provide a high standard of living for all.

In a resource-based economy all of the world's resources are held as the common heritage of all of the earth's people, thus eventually outgrowing the need for the artificial boundaries that separate people. *This is the unifying imperative.*

We must emphasize here that this approach to global governance has nothing whatever in common with the present aims of an elite to form a world government with themselves and large corporations at the helm, and the vast majority of the world's population subservient to them. Our vision of globalization empowers each and every person on the planet to be the best they can be, not to live in abject subjugation to a corporate governing body.

All social systems, regardless of political philosophy, religious beliefs, or social customs, ultimately depend upon natural resources, i.e. clean air and water, arable land and the necessary technology and personnel to maintain a high standard of living. This can be accomplished through the intelligent and humane application of science and technology. The real wealth of any nation lies in its developed and potential resources and the people who work toward the elimination of scarcity and the creation of a more humane society.

The utilization of large-scale computer based systems will assist us in defining the possible parameters required for the operation of a resource-based economy, and all construction projects would conform to environmental requirements. Over-exploitation would be unnecessary and surpassed. As of this writing NASA has announced the use of a powerful, parallel supercomputer to evaluate the global impact of national and human-induced activities on our climate.

A resource-based economy would use technology to overcome scarce resources and utilize renewable sources of energy, to computerize and automate manufacturing and inventory, and to design safe, energy-efficient cities while providing universal health care and better education. Equally importantly, it would generate a new incentive system based on human and environmental concerns.

Unfortunately science and technology have been diverted from these ends for reasons of self-interest and monetary gain through planned obsolescence, sometimes referred to as the conscious withdrawal of efficiency. For example, it is an ironic state of affairs when the U. S. Department of Agriculture, whose function is to conduct research into ways of achieving higher crop yields per acre, actually pays farmers not to produce at full capacity while many people go hungry.

In addition, we place signs next to a highway that read "Caution: Slippery When Wet," when a more effective approach would be to design a road with abrasive strips that would not be slippery. We continue to "purify" our water systems by dumping chemicals into them, despite their continuing build-up. Then again, there is the problem of the dumping of waste into rivers and waterways because it is cheaper than other, more responsible disposal methods. Yet another example is the failure of most industry to install electrostatic precipitators at their plants to prevent particulate matter from being released into the atmosphere from industrial smokestacks, a technology that has been available for over 75 years. The monetary system does not always apply known methods that would best serve people and the environment.

In our search for more, we have blinded ourselves to our personal responsibility for challenging these absurdities. A resource-based society considers us all equal shareholders of the earth who are responsible both for it and for our relationship with each other.

In a resource-based economy, the human condition is of prime concern with technology subordinate. In such an economy, production is accomplished totally by machines and the products are available to all. The concepts of "work" and "earning a living" become irrelevant. The focus is on making a life. In a resource-based economy, if the human consequences of automation are neglected, it renders all the advances of science and technology meaningless except to a selected few.

To better understand the meaning of a resource-based economy consider this: if all the money in the world suddenly disappeared, as long as topsoil, factories, and other resources were left intact, we could build anything we chose to build and fulfill any human need. *It is not money that people need, but rather it is freedom of access to the necessities of life without having to appeal to a government bureaucracy or any other agency.* In a resource-based economy money will be irrelevant. All that would be required are the resources, and the manufacturing and distribution of the products.

In a monetary system, purchasing power is not related to our capacity to produce goods and services. For example, in a recession there are computers in store windows and automobiles in car lots, but most people do not have the purchasing power to buy them.

The rules of the monetary system are obsolete and create needless strife, deprivation, and human suffering.

In today's culture of profit, we do not produce goods based on human need. We do not build houses based on population needs. We do not grow food based solely on demand, nor do we practice medicine solely to cure diseases. Industry's major motivation is profit.

Take the automobile. To service conventional automobiles today we have to remove a great deal of hardware before we can get to the engine. Why are they so complicated? Simply because ease of repair is not the concern of the manufacturers. They do not have to pay to service the car. An entire subset of the automotive industry is devoted to making a profit from the repair of cars and trucks. If manufacturers were responsible for the cost of repairs, cars and trucks would be built very differently — and with different materials and performance — with modular components easily disengaged to get at the engine.

Such construction would be typical in a resource-based economy. Many of the components in the automobile would be easily detachable to save time and energy in the rare case of repair, because no one profits by servicing automobiles or any other products. Consequently quality and simplicity of servicing and technological upgrade would be primary design drivers. Eventually, with the development of magnetically suspended bearings, lubrication and wear could be relegated to the past. There will also be proximity devices on all vehicles to prevent collisions. Automotive transport units engineered in this way would easily be service-free for many years.

This same process would be applied to all products. All industrial devices would be designed for recycling; but there would be much less recycling when we build household materials and products of superior quality that are designed not to wear out or break down.

A resource-based world economy would also involve all-out efforts to develop new, clean, and renewable sources of energy: geothermal; controlled fusion; solar; photovoltaic; wind, wave, and tidal power; and even fuel from the oceans. We would eventually be able to have energy in unlimited quantity that could propel civilization for thousands of years. A resource-based economy must also be committed to the redesign of our cities, transportation systems, and industrial plants, allowing them to be energy efficient, clean, and conveniently serve the needs of all people.

All shipping and transportation systems would maintain a balanced load economy, fully utilized in both directions. There would be no empty trucks, trains, or transport units on return trips. There would be no freight trains stored in yards dependent on the business cycle for their use.

What else would a resource-based economy mean? Technology intelligently and efficiently applied, conserves energy, reduces waste, and provides more leisure time. With automated inventory on a global scale we can maintain a balance between production and distribution. Planned obsolescence would be unnecessary and non-existent in a resource-based economy. All packaging systems would be standardized, requiring less storage space and easy handling. Only nutritious and healthy food would be available. To eliminate waste from impermanent products, such as newsprint, books and magazines, a light-sensitive film can be placed over a monitor or TV to produce a temporary printout of the news of the day or any other relevant information. This material will be capable of holding the information until it is deleted. This would conserve millions of pounds of paper, a major part of the recycling process. Eventually most of the paperwork, including the transfer of money, would be eliminated.

As we outgrow the need for professions based on the monetary system, for instance those of lawyer, banker, insurance agent, advertiser, salesperson, and stockbroker, a considerable amount of waste will be eliminated. Considerable amount of energy would also be saved by eliminating the duplication of competitive products such as tools, eating utensils, pots and pans, vacuum cleaners and those 300 wrenches mentioned earlier. Choice is good. But instead of hundreds of different manufacturing plants and all the paperwork and personnel required to turn out similar products, only a few of the highest quality would be needed to serve the entire population.

Our only shortage is the lack of creative thought and intelligence in ourselves and our elected leaders to solve these problems. The most valuable, untapped resource today is human ingenuity. With the elimination of debt, the fear of losing one's job will no longer be a threat This assurance, combined with education on how to relate to people in a much more meaningful way, could considerably reduce both mental and physical stress and leave us free to explore and develop our abilities.

If the thought of eliminating money still troubles you, consider this: If a group of people with gold, demons and money were stranded on an island that had no resources, their wealth would be irrelevant to their survival. It is only when resources are scarce that money can be used to control their distribution. One could not, for example, sell the air we breathe or water abundantly flowing down from a mountain stream. Although air and water are valuable, in abundance they cannot be sold.

Money is only important in a society when certain resources for survival must be rationed and the people accept money as an exchange medium for the scarce resources. Money is a social convention, an agreement if you will. It is neither a natural resource nor does it represent one. It is not necessary for survival unless we have been conditioned to accept it as such.

WHAT WILL MOTIVATE PEOPLE?

Some people claim the free-enterprise system and its competition create incentive. This is only partially true. It also perpetuates greed, embezzlement, corruption, crime, stress, and economic hardship and insecurity. Most of our major developments in science and technology resulted from the efforts of very few individuals, working independently and often against great opposition: Goddard, Galileo, Darwin, Tesla, Edison, Einstein, etc. These individuals were also genuinely concerned with solving problems and improving processes, rather than with mere financial gain. Despite our slavish belief that money is incentive, we often mistrust those whose sole motivation is monetary gain. This can be said for doctors, lawyers, and those in just about any field.

If the basic necessities are accessible, what will motivate us? Quite simply, the things we care about. Children reared in affluent environments, in which food, clothing, shelter, nutrition, extensive education and much more are provided, still demonstrate incentive and initiative. On the other hand, there is overwhelming evidence to support the fact that malnutrition, lack of employment, minimum wage, poor health, a lack of direction, lack of education, homelessness, little or no reinforcement for one's efforts, poor role models, poverty, and a bleak prospect for the future can and do destroy incentive and the drive to achieve.

The aim of our new social design is to encourage a new incentive system, one that is no longer directed toward the shallow and self-centered goals of wealth, property, and power. These new incentives would encourage people toward self-fulfillment and creativity, the elimination of scarcity, the protection of the environment, and most of all concern for their fellow human beings.

The air we breathe, clean water, sunshine, forests, and the totality of nature for the most part support life without charge. Provided with good nutrition in a highly productive humane society, people will evolve a new incentive system. Without the need to work to survive, there would be so many new things to explore and invent that the notion of people sitting around and doing nothing is just absurd. The lack of incentive in our present culture occurs when people dare not dream of a future that seems unattainable to them.

Each phase of social evolution creates its own incentive system. In primitive times the incentive to hunt for food was generated by hunger; the incentive to create a javelin or a bow and arrow evolved as a process supportive to the hunt. With the advent of the agrarian revolution the motivation for hunting was no longer relevant, and incentives shifted to the cultivation of crops and supporting implements, the domestication of animals, and protection of personal property. In a civilization where people receive food, medical care, education, and housing, incentives would again change appropriately. People would be free to explore other possibilities and lifestyles that could not be anticipated in earlier times.

The nature of incentive and motivation depends on many factors. We know, for example, that an individual's physical and mental health directly relates to that person's level of motivation and productivity, as we are also aware of the fact that all healthy babies are naturally inquisitive. In India and other areas of great and continuing scarcity many people are motivated against the accumulation of wealth and material property. So, they renounce all worldly goods. Under those conditions this is not difficult. This would seem to be in direct conflict with western culture's emphasis on the accumulation of material wealth. Yet, which is more valid? Your answer to this question would depend upon your culturally influenced value-system.

Some people overcome the shortcomings of their environment in spite of an apparent lack of positive reinforcements. They provide their own "self-reinforcement", are able to see an improvement in whatever it is they are engaged in, and achieve an intrinsic sense of accomplishment. Their reinforcement does not depend on the approval of others. Those children who do depend on the approval of a group tend to have low self-esteem. Children who do not depend on group approval acquire a sense of self-esteem by improving upon their performance.

Throughout history, many innovators, artists, and inventors have been ruthlessly exploited, ridiculed, and abused while receiving very little financial incentive. Yet, they endured such hardship because they were motivated to learn and to discover new ways of doing things. On the other hand, Leonardo da Vinci, Michelangelo, and Beethoven, to name a few of history's most creative minds, received the generous sponsorship of wealthy patrons. Yet this did not kill their incentive in the least; on the contrary, these individuals strove to reach new heights of creativity, perseverance and individual accomplishment. Creativity is often its own motivation

This is a difficult concept to grasp because most of us have been brought up with a set of notions about the way that we ought to think and behave. These are based upon ancient ideas that are actually irrelevant today. To a limited extent, some primitive cultures in remote islands in the South Pacific have full access to all the food they require and to clean water and air. There is probably no question that most of them are far better adjusted than many people in the so-called civilized world. There is no evidence that demonstrates that unlimited access to the necessities of life diminishes incentive.

It has often been stated that war spurs creativity. This deliberately falsified concept has no basis in fact. It is the increased government financing of the war industries that helps develop so many new materials and inventions. There is no question a saner society would be able to create a more constructive incentive system if our knowledge of the factors that shape human motivation were applied.

Experimental psychologists have shown that the environment plays a major role in shaping our behavior and values. If constructive behavior is appropriately rewarded during early childhood, the child becomes motivated to repeat the rewarded behavior, provided the reinforcement meets the individual needs of the child. For example, a football given to a child who is interested in botany would not be a reward from the child's point of view. It is very unfortunate that so many individuals in our society today are not appropriately rewarded for their creative behavior.

In a resource-based economy, motivation and incentive will be encouraged through recognition of, and concern for, the needs of the individual. This means providing the necessary environment, educational facilities, good nutrition, health care, warmth, love, and security that people require.

LOVE AND EXTENSIONALITY

For centuries love has been a dominant word in our vocabulary. The definition varies so much today that the word has become almost meaningless. Love is subject to many different interpretations, most of them irrelevant to the behavior associated with it. Perhaps the word love may one day be redefined in much more relevant terms, such as our being *extensional* to one another. What is being extensional? Our arms and hands enable us to pick up and rotate objects, to view them from many different positions. Our arms and hands are extensional devices along with our eyes, ears, nose and our entire physical body.

When a single individual tries to build a log cabin, it may take considerable time to complete. With the help of several neighbors this job can be completed in a relatively short time. The neighbors become very extensional to this individual. The same is true with an entire community that acts in a supportive manner towards one another.

In the physical sciences a structural engineer has to work with the metallurgist to help improve the strength and quality of structural materials. The two and their skills, their teamwork, are genuinely extensional. The physical sciences are the closet approach to genuine extensionality. Rather than being directed at a single individual, genuine extensionality serves all people equally. For instance, when contaminated water is purified, it benefits any person that utilizes the process. Vaccinating children to prevent disease is not only extensional to the individual but to almost everyone that they come in contact with. Identifying conditions responsible for a disease is extensional and beneficial to all people regardless of their personal values and philosophy.

When different nations share their technology intelligently, it is extensional to all people regardless of their independent beliefs and national interests. Corporate systems, however, chiefly benefit the owners and the shareholders. When inventions serve the needs of all people they will truly be extensional.

To know the difference between governments and people that merely verbalize good intentions as opposed to displaying actual extensionality is essential to advancing civilization both physically and intellectually.

When a bank lends money to an individual there is a benefit from this but this comes at a cost called debt and obligation. Genuine extensionality does not extract a toll. Extensionality at its most basic is a simple act of kindness that one does without any debt being incurred by the other person.

The more people become extensional to one another, the richer the civilization and the interaction between individuals becomes. In the future, instead of asking "Do I love this person?" one might instead identify the specific areas of extensionality that one shares with them.

WOULD ALL THE PEOPLE IN SUCH A CYBERNATED SOCIETY BE UNIFORM?

Yes, in many ways, they would. For example, everyone would possess an understanding of the importance of extending maximum courtesy to all nations and to one another. They would share an intense curiosity for all that is new and challenging. With a better understanding people could possess a flexibility of outlook unknown in previous times, free of bigotry and prejudice. In addition, the people of this new society would care for their fellow human beings and for the protection, maintenance, and stewardship of the Earth's natural environment. Additionally, everyone — regardless of race, color, or creed — would have equal access to all of the amenities that this innovative culture could supply.

SOMETHING FOR NOTHING

Some people question the morality of receiving something for nothing. Once when I was speaking at a college a student expressed opposition to the idea of getting something for nothing. I asked if he would answer a personal question and when he replied, yes, I asked him "Are you paying your way through school or are you parents?" He admitted his parents were. I pointed out that if he really did believe people should not receive something for nothing then in the event of the death of a family member he would prefer the inheritance be left to the heart or cancer fund, rather than passing to him. Needless to say, the students were opposed to this idea.

Merely being born in a developed country, we have access to many things we put no effort toward, such as the telephone, the automobile, electricity, and running water. These gifts of human ingenuity and invention do not degrade our lives, but rather enrich us. What degrades us is our lack of concern for those unfortunate enough to experience poverty, hunger, lack of medical care, and war. The social designs that are proposed in this writing merely provide the opportunity for individuals to develop their fullest potential in whatever endeavor they choose without the fear of any loss of individuality.

WHAT GUARANTIES PEOPLE THE RIGHT OF PARTICIPATION?

There is always a reason for corruption and that is that someone gets something they consider valuable out of it. Without vested interests or the use of money, there is little to be gained by squelching opinion, falsifying information or taking advantage of anyone. There are no underlying, rigid social barriers to limit the participation of anyone or restrain the introduction of new ideas. The main objective is full access to information and the delivering of goods and services to all people, a state of affairs that will enable people to be prepared to participate in the exciting challenges of this new society.

HOW WOULD RESOURCES BE DISTRIBUTED EQUITABLY IN A RESOURCE-BASED SOCIETY?

Distribution of goods and services without the use of money or tokens would be accomplished through the establishment of distribution centers. These distribution centers would be similar to expositions, where the advantages of new products could be explained and demonstrated. For example, if you visited Yellowstone National Park you could check out a camera or camcorder, use it and then return it to another distribution center or drop-off, eliminating storing and maintenance.

Besides the computerized centers throughout the various communities where products would eventually be displayed, there will be 3-D, flat-screen imaging capabilities in each home. If you desire an item, an order can be placed and the item automatically delivered directly to your place of residence. All raw materials for the manufacture of these products can be transported directly to the manufacturing facilities by automated transportation "sequences" such as boats, monorails, mag-lev trains, pipelines, and pneumatic tubes. An automated inventory system would be connected to both the distribution centers and the manufacturing facilities, thus coordinating production to meet demand and providing a constant evaluation of preferences and consumption. In this way a balanced-load economy can be maintained. Shortages, over-runs, and waste could be eliminated.

IN CONCLUSION

Despite today's National Security mania for intruding on everyone's privacy, in a resource-based economy no one need take from another. It will be considered socially offensive and counterproductive for machines to monitor the activities of human beings, but more to the point, there will be no reason for it. The main concern of this new social arrangement is to create an environment that will encourage the widest range of individuality, creativity, constructive endeavor and cooperation without any kind of elitism, technical or otherwise. Most significantly, a resource-based economy would generate a far different incentive system, one based on human and environmental concern. This would not be a uniform culture but one that is designed to be in a constant process of growth and improvement.

It also advocates the stabilizing of the world's population through education, until such a point as the human population coincides with the earth's carrying capacity. Only when population exceeds the productive capacity of the land do many problems such as greed, crime, and violence emerge.

As we enhance the lives of others, protect our environment, and work toward abundance, all our lives can become richer and more secure. If these values were put into practice, it would enable all of us to achieve a much higher standard of living within a relatively short period of time — a standard of living that would be continuously improved.

In the society of the future, when the monetary system and scarcity are replaced by a resource-based economy and most of our needs are met, private ownership as we know it would cease. The concept of ownership would be of no advantage whatsoever in a high-energy society.

Although this is difficult for many to imagine, even the wealthiest person today would be immensely better off in a high-energy, resource-based society. Today the middle classes live better than kings of times past. In a resource-based economy everyone would live far better than the powerful and wealthy of today.

People would be free to pursue whatever constructive field of endeavor they chose, without any of the economic pressures, restraints, and taxation that are inherent in the monetary system. By constructive endeavor, we mean anything that enhances the lives of the individual and others. When education and resources are available to all without a price tag, there will be no limit to the human potential. With these major alterations people would eventually be able to live longer, more meaningful and healthier lives. The measure of success would be based on the fulfillment of one's individual pursuits rather than on the acquisition of wealth, property, and power.

This proposal is neither Utopian nor Orwellian, nor does it reflect the dreams of impractical idealists. Instead, it offers attainable goals requiring only the intelligent application of what we already know. The only limitations are those which we impose upon ourselves.

CHAPTER 8

THE NEXT PHASE OF EVOLUTION: MACHINE INTELLIGENCE

WELCOME TO THE AGE OF AUTOMATION AND AI

AUTOMATION IS A MAJOR PART OF OUR LIVES. By replacing human labor and intelligence with machines, we achieved a standard of living unknown even to royalty in past times. Automation and its more recent partner, cybernation, or the wedding of the computer to production, has unleashed an outflow of goods and services never before experienced. The next step, underway now, adds artificial intelligence (AI) — computer programming that attempts to simulate human attributes of decision-making and hypothesis testing along with self-correction. AI redesigns mechanical and electronic systems to simulate and improve upon human performance. As exciting as these developments are, they are only the beginning.

The way we conduct human affairs is being challenged by the introduction of computers. The Internet and the World Wide Web are providing the groundwork for the evolution of a new social direction in human interaction, bringing together vast stores of information from many different disciplines.

From the comfort of our homes, schools, offices and libraries we are now able to instantly access a world of information on the Internet and World Wide Web, interacting with people throughout the world. Current electronic mail and messaging systems reach Australia as quickly as the office next door. This extremely rapid, easy communication process changes radically how we relate to each other and how we conduct business. Information flows across the net statelessly — ignoring customs, borders, and international agreements. To those formerly wedded to the control of information, these are terrifying times.

Other developments in nanotechnology and replication offer humanity the opportunity to command its destiny to a degree never before achieved, to overcome scarcity once and for all, and to virtually eliminate poverty, unnecessary human suffering, deprivation, and perhaps even the need for work.

Where will this lead us? Will human beings eventually be replaced by the efficiency of machines? What will we do? How will we make a living?

As some fear, will machines enhanced by artificial intelligence eventually take over? Will people indeed become obsolete?

In this chapter, we probe the possibilities of the future of automation — its promise and its dangers. Through it all, bear in mind that these mechanical children can so far do only what we humans program them to do. For all their sophistication, they have none of our ambitions or failings; nor are they likely to. It is, therefore, our decision whether we use them to elevate people everywhere — or to serve our fears, prejudices, and power seeking. Therein lies our future, and the future of our technology.

For the first time in history, we have access to the information and training necessary to take charge of our own destiny. We are also fully responsible for the decisions we make and their consequences. Do we have the capacity, the will, and the intelligence to clearly think out and implement changes for our overall benefit, or will we wait for some catastrophic event to direct the future course?

For any society to improve the quality of life for its people, it must overcome the rigidity of the present. Science and technology undergo continuous modification and revision, whereas social customs, values and mores tend to remain fairly static. If the outmoded, unquestioning and emotion-driven methods used by our government and economic systems today had been applied to the sciences, we would have made very little technological progress.

The greatest fear people have regarding the coming age of cybernation is that millions will be left behind, unable to adjust to or understand the way the new culture operates. In fact, some people do fall behind or are slow to catch up during times of change. Most of us do not understand the science and technology behind the product we already use. Fewer and fewer of us work on our own cars. Not many people repair their own home computers, refrigerators or TV's. We have neither the training, the tools, nor the time to do so. But one of the interesting aspects of the new technologies is that you do not need understanding to use it. The human interface portion is so simple that former third world nations have easily made the jump from horse-drawn plows to computers — and many are now leading developers of software.

The history of invention includes all systems that enabled human beings to improve communication beyond the first, most primitive grunts. Books, radio, television, and all other forms of human communication extended our relationship to other human beings and added to our range of consciousness. The computer, like all other inventions, tends to serve as an extension of human consciousness, a brain outside of our bodies, yet indirectly connected to our nervous system, the world, and eventually the stars. The development of the electronic computer, World Wide Web and the Internet have liberated the user from many of the limitations imposed on them by governments. It is no longer a simple process for nations to shield their citizens from controversial ideas.

Although we are at the very early stages of the Internet the only existing threat to this new, unintended liberator is the attempt to control input and output of information. In fact, some already want limitations imposed on material regarded — often subjectively — as being objectionable. Once established, any such control may be gradually extended to all areas that might threaten an existing power structure. The conditions that perpetuate these threats may not be a direct conspiracy, but the result of thousands of self-appointed guardians of the status quo.

Eventually, all social systems must extend beyond current boundaries and nationalities and achieve linkage, in order to arrive at a long-term, sustainable future for generations to come. In a relatively short time, most people will realize that a cybernated society may have a more beneficial potential for all humanity than any other invention in history. *Here we do not speak of the use of technology to advance the self-interests of transnational corporations, but to organize a global economy based on human rights and basic human needs.* This new world of both human and computer-generated directives can provide us with alternative strategies for global policies, part of a joint venture in problem-solving for the benefit of all the earth's inhabitants.

Automated machines today can conceivably perform almost any task accomplished by human beings. Since we have only two hands, machines have been designed that will far exceed the manipulative ability of any human being. As far back as 1961, U.S. industries announced that they had developed the first general-purpose automation machine at a price of around $2,500. It was called the TransfeRobot. Its swinging arm and hand were infinitely superior to any human arm or hand at a given task. It never tired and the electronic brain guiding it was not prone to wandering attention. It picked things up and put things down with an accuracy of two thousandths of an inch. In 1961 the Westclox Co. of LaSalle, Illinois used the TransfeRobot to oil clock assemblies as they sped by on a conveyor belt. It oiled eight precision bearings in a second.

Interestingly enough, this same year a U. S. Senate subcommittee on technology and automation revealed its observation that, considering the extent of automation, the total amount of goods and services required by the entire country could now be provided by ten percent of the work force that existed at that time. Ninety percent of the workforce no longer provided critical goods and products. Essentially, then, as long ago as 1961, 90% of the workforce toiled for non-essential goods and services. So-called service industries and work related to controlling and managing the use of money took the place of producing food and clothing.

The advent of cybernation could be regarded as the only real emancipation proclamation for humankind if used humanely and intelligently. Cybernation could enable people to have the highest conceivable standard of living with practically no labor. It could free people for the first time from a highly structured and outwardly imposed routine of repetitive day-by-day activity. It could permit one to actually live the Greek concept of leisure, where slaves did most of the work and citizens had time to cultivate their minds. The essential difference will lie in the fact that in the future, each of us will command more than a million slaves — but these will be mechanical and electrical slaves that will end forever the degrading use of any human being to do, against their will, the work of another. Perhaps the greatest aid in enhancing the survival of the human race is the introduction of the electronic computer and artificial intelligence, which may very well save the human race from its own inadequacies.

As we begin building our requirements and plan for a new human society, we need commonly accepted values for clean air, water, and other elements of self-sustainment. These, along with a complete inventory of the earth's resources, will form the basis for a holistic approach to cybernated decision-making. Any change recommended by cybernated systems can also provide a great deal of information on the effects that innovative systems will have upon the entire system.

This is not a project for the distant future. Some of this work is already well under way.

The father of cybernation, Dr. Norbert Wiener, had this to say of the emerging age of non-human work: "It is a degradation to a human being to chain them to an oar and use them as a source of power, but it is almost an equal degradation to assign them to purely repetitive tasks in a factory which demands less than a millionth of their brain power." What dreams, what goals will we be able to achieve when we have the time to pursue them?

DEMISE OF THE MONETARY SYSTEM

Government and industry will continue to assign more and more responsibility for decision making to intelligent machines. Today's machines handle trillions of bits of information per second — far more than is manageable by any number of industrial or political decision-makers. They can also assemble and assign constantly updated information.

The other side of this trend is that so many people will be replaced, we will no longer have the purchasing power needed to sustain a monetary-based system that burdens the entire population and government with insurmountable debt.

As the old monetary system begins to displace more and more people by its reliance on automation, these people will cease to respect the authority of industry. The time-honored pattern of living in all industrial countries, the balancing of work and family interest, would become impossible to maintain for the majority of people displaced by automation.

When automation and cybernation are utilized to their fullest potential, not only industrial workers but also most professionals will be replaced by machines. It may surprise people when life-like, computer-generated images replace actors, entertainers, and television announcers as well. The movie Final Fantasy, released in 2001, featured an entirely computer-generated cast.

Even the most visionary speculative writers and futurists of the twentieth century would have had difficulties accepting the possibility of robots replacing surgeons, engineers, top management, airline pilots and other professionals. It is not unthinkable that machines may one day write novels or poems, compose music, and eventually replace humans in government and in the management of world affairs.

This is not a discussion about the morality and ethics of human participation, but a straightforward description of future technological trends. Nature does not subscribe to human interpretations of good or evil, or hang onto traits or species that are no longer useful. Nature operates without any concern whatsoever for the previous structures of living plants and organisms, many of which have been superseded again and again. There are no permanent structures in nature, although many human beings would like to believe otherwise, especially when it comes to their own species.

Although the technical changes of the future would be far beyond anything we could imagine today, the most profound effects would not be in the new technologies but rather in the many different ways that we conduct our lives and social institutions. As we move toward a more cybernated world, most people will no longer be needed to manage and operate this emerging civilization. Most of the world's fragmented social systems will be supported by a network of computerized centers and operations.

Today computers and AI are not capable of advising management with the most appropriate direction to take to maintain the competitive edge. Information regarding other corporate practices is not always known. In order for industries to maintain the competitive edge they cannot share their industrial processes, production techniques or business plans. Even if they did, a railway strike could stop their shipping ability. Predictability is often outside of their control. It is difficult to plan unless society controls a great many variables

Eventually, interlinked cyber-centers will coordinate the service industries, transportation systems, public health care and education with the latest data and the state of the world economy. Interdisciplinary teams of men and women comprised of systems engineers, computer programmers, systems analysts, researchers and the like could supervise, manage, and analyze the effectiveness of the flow of goods and services.

Such a world, linked together by communication networks and continuous flow lines of information and services, will provide a much higher standard of living to all people. Although today the consequence of automation and AI applied in a monetary base world economy often results in a much higher standard of living, it is only to a relatively small number of people. The advantages of newer technologies have not yet been made available to everyone.

Today most people look upon computers as being simply another, clever addition to technology, yet this facet of technology is now evolving to bring about the greatest force for social change we have yet encountered, allowing us an ever-widening range of decision-making in government, medicine, and industry. All indications are that AI will result in more significant changes for the human race than did any previous breakthrough or revolution.

As early as 1971, a single space satellite sent back to earth 400 miles of tape data that would take five competent analysts about 500 years to decipher and convert into useful information. We are rapidly approaching the time when human intelligence will be incapable of simulating the technological complexities necessary to manage a highly advanced society. Existing technologies are rapidly exceeding the human capacity to absorb and process essential information. The human mind is far too slow and simplistic a structure to handle the forthcoming information surge. We have neither the training nor the capability to handle the trillions of bits of information per second necessary to efficiently manage the new advances.

That is why we urgently advocate a society that utilizes cybernetics not merely as a system of tabulation and measurement, but as a way to process vital information and channel it for the benefit of all humankind. Only our most capable computers can store and sort through the multitude of data necessary to arrive at equitable and sustainable decision analysis for the development and distribution of resources on a global scale.

In this cybernated global economy, mega machines directed by sophisticated AI will excavate canals, dig tunnels, and construct bridges, viaducts and dams — all based on designs that accommodate human and animal migrations and ecological dependencies — without the necessity of human involvement. Human participation will be in the form of selecting the desired ends. Human labor would no longer be required. In this society, construction techniques would be vastly different from those employed today. Self-erecting structures would prove most expedient and efficient in the construction of industrial plants, bridges, buildings and eventually the entire global infrastructure. This would not create cookie-cutter cities: the notion that large-scale, overall planning implies mass uniformity is absurd. Cities would be uniform only to the degree that they would require far less materials, save time and energy, and yet be flexible enough to allow for innovative changes, while maintaining the highest quality possible to support the local ecology — both human and environmental. Utilizing technology in this way would make it possible for a global society to achieve social advancement and worldwide reconstruction in the shortest time possible.

Eventually factories would be designed by robots for robots; the cybernated systems could also be self-programming by means of environmental feedback. Machines would be capable of self-replication and improvement of their operational range, while at the same time repairing themselves and updating their own circuitry. Since the computers and systems involved would be continuously self-monitoring, parts could be supplied and installed well in advance of any wear. The machines could operate continuously except when conducting their own maintenance and repair. In a resource-based economy, all the work of robots would be directed toward the well being of human beings. In such a society monitoring of people by machines would serve no useful purpose, except where deliberate human feedback was needed.

As artificial intelligence develops, machines will be assigned the tasks of complex decision-making in industrial, military and governmental affairs. **This would not imply a take-over by machines.** Instead it would be a gradual transfer of decision-making processes to machine intelligence as the next phase of social evolution.

This automated control could come into being when sensors that monitor the resources of the earth to support human activity are installed in every conceivable location, linked through a worldwide network of computers. Unlike the current trend toward policing human behavior, these benign monitors would serve the sole purpose of allowing us to arrive at the most appropriate decisions for both human and environmental benefit. I must state again that monitoring of personal behavior will be neither necessary nor desirable.

Artificial intelligence is already applied by industry in such areas as the monitoring of weather patterns by satellite, production control, and automation. With the further development of computerized systems, these environmental sensors and extensors can provide the necessary feedback to help us carefully determine each successive stage and develop the required analytical and decision-making tools. The degree to which such computerized systems are effective would be based upon the amount of sensors they were equipped with. We must always include the possibility of unforeseen variables in the environment such as fire, flood, hurricanes, earthquake, and other natural and man-made disasters.

An example of the tremendous potential of cybernated sensing systems may be seen in a hotel of the future. In the rare event of a fire, an audio-visual alarm instantly appears on the room's TV screen. The screen would then display a 3-D image and audio message, describing the route to take to avoid the fire. When exiting the building an illuminated line could indicate the way out.

The probable future of robotics is that the machines will undergo radical changes in their physical appearance and performance. They will behave more like living systems and be capable of making appropriate decisions within their sphere of operation. In the event of any unforeseen threat or danger to humans, they will act on our behalf. To maximize reliability and minimize the possibility of system failure, all computers can be programmed with a degree of flexibility and capable of automatic shutdown in the event of failure of any one of their parts.

It is irrational to fear machines in this benign role. Some people are concerned that there is too much emphasis on technology in this proposal. In fact, it is concern for humanity has inspired me to initiate these ideas for the redesign of a culture and to apply the best of science and technology to enhance the lives of everyone. We must keep in mind that it is not automated technology or machines we should be wary of, but rather the abuse and misuse of this technology by selfish interests. We can build rockets to explore outer space and to enhance the quality of life on Earth, or we can use them to destroy other nations. Ultimately, it is people who decide what ends these inanimate machines will serve. The aim of this social design is to apply advanced technology to produce abundance and improve the quality of life for all.

To reach a decision, intelligent people acquire information from appropriate sources and behave accordingly. Unfortunately, in the pursuit of advantage, humans acquire and route information for personal and corporate gain. Cybernated systems programmed for common concerns will do much to prevent unchecked, executive authority or abuses of power. In a resource-based, cybernated system, all decisions are based upon direct environmental, human and industrial feedback from all the cities, factories, warehouses, distribution facilities, and transportation networks. All the decisions are appropriate to the greater needs of society, rather than to those of the corporate interests.

Although many people claim to feel very uncomfortable about machines making decisions, everyone demands a weighing scale be used when purchasing any quantifiable amount of goods. To preclude a power failure in a hospital, people expect back-up emergency generators that automatically switch on with the least amount of inconvenience to the staff and patients. We are so used to machines making decisions about climate control, directing traffic lights, answering our phones, forwarding our messages, managing our calendars and the like, that we no longer consider them remarkable. Today people want and expect many aspects of modern life to be handled seamlessly and invisibly by so-called "intelligent machine decisions".

Few people think about or know how machines make decisions. Instead when additional machine use is proposed, they project their own personal agendas and emotions into the machine design. While some people proclaim their fear of machines, there has never been a single, deliberate act or plan by machines to hurt anyone. Unfortunately, the same cannot be said of human beings. Humans, not machines, use nerve gas and missiles to destroy. Even automobile accidents are mostly caused by human beings, rather than by mechanical failures — and even mechanical failures can often be traced back to human error.

It is easy to understand how readily we might accept computer decisions when we consider possibilities such as this: a man, leaving the top down in a convertible, feels a few raindrops and must pull over to raise the top, although it would be more convenient to have a system of sensors installed in the car that would raise the top automatically when rain begins. One sensor detects the raindrops, another scans the car to ensure no fingers or pets t could be injured by the mechanism automatically putting up the top and side windows. This, and much more, is technically feasible. The question that remains is: how smart do you wish your car to be?

Another example, designed and patented by the author, is a lightweight net installed at the bottom of a swimming pool. If a child falls into the pool, the net is activated to come up from the bottom of the pool saving the child if the parents or guardian are inattentive. When no one is using the pool the net remains at the surface. The net requires no human decision. The net's computer reacts to feedback from the environment.

Humans will still be relevant in this new society. After all, by and for whom are these machines designed?

Only in a cybernated world can decisions be based on the full range of relevant data available, without interference from human ego or self-interest. This could eventually provide us with the best solutions at the time to most social problems.

Today the majority of problems in computerized systems result from flawed human intervention. Computers will eventually be capable enough to design their own programs, improve and repair their own circuitry, and update information relevant to social needs.

Almost all life forms of the past — plants, animals, and even humanoid forms — have been replaced through the process of evolution. There are no permanent structures in nature. The assumption that the human being is the final product of evolution is based upon a narrow, self-centered projection. The human being is not a separate, self-sufficient entity: it is integrated into and dependent on nature to survive.

It is arrogant and unrealistic for us to believe that man is the final product of evolution. More and more, we see the merging of human ingenuity with machine intelligence. How many lives have been helped by the use of artificial limbs, joints, hearts, skin, and so forth? How much pure information, uncluttered by human frailties, is processed by computers every day? The next stage of evolution must surely be the merging of biological systems with man-made systems.

It takes many millions of years for living organisms to evolve, and additional thousands of years to shed vestigial organs. The human increased in size and complexity due to the many new convolutions in its neuronal development. The enlargement of the brain accompanied a corresponding increase in the capacity for associative memory.

The development of electronic systems required a different "evolution". Early computers were huge — room-sized — but now capability of information storage systems increases while the hardware occupies less and less space. Another major difference in technology is that non-functioning parts are eliminated or replaced immediately. In human systems old ideas may be retained far beyond their usefulness and new ideas shunned. In artificial intelligence and computerized systems information is updated rapidly, appropriately and constantly. Today it takes years to transfer acquired knowledge to another person, whereas in computerized systems information can be transferred instantaneously to an entire global network.

Most of us cling tenaciously to our old habits of thought, but technological progress has little use for custom and tradition. Human systems are subject to neural lag, and tend to revert to the familiar. Neural lag may be defined as the tendency to resist forming new and more appropriate associative patterns in favor of old, familiar ones. For example, during the early stages of automotive development, a statue of a horse's head was mounted to the front hood, and the rear portion of the car retained a coachman's seat.

In the field of electronics, if neural lag had prevailed, the industry would have failed to achieve its many technological innovations. To remain at the forefront of technology one must be capable of updating one's methods, discarding outdated technology, and examining new paradigms.

When we examine our present social design we find that it does not keep up with the rate of change required to take advantage of this accelerated pace of information and innovation. The person of today thinks in terms of having to get a job in order to support himself and his family. With the limitless possibilities of our technology today, this could be considered an example of neural lag. The adherence to a mentality of scarcity is another.

No matter how strong our fear or resentment of social cybernation, the process is already underway. In all branches of industry, medicine, agriculture, and technology computers are being assigned the role of decision-making. As we outgrow the need for human participation, whether it be in the military, the marketplace, or eventually government, more and more tasks will be assigned to artificial intelligence.

Although all politicians, decision-makers, educators, humanists and the literary community will probably resist this level of cybernation, the greatest level of resistance will come from the general public, attuned as they are to being directed by other humans for thousands of years.

And yet cybernation will prevail. As an old Chinese proverb has it: *The dogs may howl at the moon, but the moon will continue on its honorable journey.*

MACHINE EMOTIONS IN A CYBERNATED SOCIETY

Let us look at the concept of human emotions in machines. Imagine an automobile with computerized emotions linked to built-in, feedback mechanisms. This car is equipped with a pendulum under the hood that when an abrupt turn is made prompts it to respond via its speaker system, "What are you trying to do, destroy the car and everyone in it? Where did you learn to drive? Have you no regard for others?"

Worse yet, what if the car suddenly decided it didn't like you in the middle of that abrupt turn?

Of course, this is preposterous. And yet, how often does such an approach fail when we use it in an attempt to modify the behavior of others?

What purpose, indeed, would emotions serve if incorporated into the design of intelligent machines? Machines have no emotions. They do not feel ambition, love or hate. They do not seek power over people or harbor any repressed desire to harm or enslave anyone. They will never make demands on their users or seek revenge if misused. They will not hold a grudge, complain or manifest guile or deceit. These are flawed human traits.

With no understanding of or sensitivity to human emotions such as love and trust, machines guide aircraft, ships and spacecraft to their destinations and make the appropriate decisions to avoid troublesome weather conditions. With no concept of charity, the machines provide an abundance of food and preserve it by refrigeration. They heat and cool our homes. They sound alarms in the event of fire, warn us when hurricanes and tornadoes threaten. They order parts for machines before they wear out. Although they do not hold the hand of a distressed person, they warn us about toxic gasses in the environment.

Perhaps human emotions would be the only attribute, if given a choice, which machine technology would reject outright. When one thinks about it, the fact that machines have no emotions may in some ways make them superior to human systems — certainly so when the task requires immediate response and dispassionate weighing of options.

We could put pressure sensors in automobile tires so that they would be able to maintain their own required pressure with a built-in pump. We could program them to slow down automatically to 15 mph when their monitors detect a school zone. If there is a child or pet behind the car when backing up, the car would automatically stop.

It makes more sense to design built-in standards of performance that operate the car, rather than indulge in the useless exercise of trying to alter the behavior of the driver with verbal abuse or stern admonitions. This same system could be applied to all aspects of the electrical, mechanical, and computerized cybernated world of the future, including human communication.

It is not a matter of the machine "caring" about the results of its actions. It is a matter of designing the function of safety into the machine. It is not emotions that are needed by machines — it is responsibility to the humans they serve. What we require of them is the ability to act intelligently with respect to human welfare and make the appropriate responses to a wide range of situations. If all of this could be accomplished without emotions, does this not raise some interesting questions about a number of human emotions?

NANOTECHNOLOGY TO COME

Nanotechnology will eventually control and direct the building of molecular structures, atom by atom, into any molecular configuration we desire. By means of such a process we will be able to rearrange matter and eliminate all shortages forever.

With the application of sophisticated technologies such as atomic and molecular replication, we might be able to reengineer the natural processes with advanced robotic manipulators that utilize phase array teletactile communication. 'Phase array' refers to the control and manipulation of light to generate three-dimensional images that appear solid. 'Teletactile' refers to the ability to impart the sensation of solidity and touch to a merely *transmitted* object. This advanced form of tele-communication will create a virtual simulation one can see, feel, hear, smell and touch.

Although such instantaneous technologies may be difficult for most to comprehend today, it is no more than an extension of current technologies, and similar to the way that color television images can be transmitted to any part of the world today. The major difference is that the image and sound will be transmitted three-dimensionally and feel solid to the touch.

The step beyond involves directly replicating an object, rather than merely simulating it. On earth, this might be accomplished instantaneously and could eventually eliminate the necessity of our cumbersome system of transporting objects from place to place by land, air, or water. Beyond the earth, it could be the future transport system from one planet or galaxy to another. Such space transportation, though achieving speeds inconceivable by present standards, would likely not be instantaneous, the rate of travel depending on the distance of the transmission.

As nanotechnology advances, machines could have a transmorphic capability, able to change their shape to the most efficient form to accomplish any given task. Such machines could constantly assess conditions as they perform their tasks and "morph" into a more appropriate configuration as necessary.

To help understand this process, imagine evolution as a series of rapid successions, as opposed to the millions of years it takes to accomplish organic changes. Machines as described above could instantaneously rearrange their molecular structures to best serve human needs.

Of course, such machines will not look like conventional machines, any more than a microchip looks like a phonograph record. They would be as different from our present concepts of machines as humans differ from primordial life forms. Today, living systems conform to the world by natural process or they perish. In the future, machine systems will adjust the world according to the specifications set by an emerging culture, a culture that will, hopefully, be dedicated to universal human and environmental well-being.

THE DOWNSIZING OF THE GODS

AI will eventually supplant antiquated notions about gods and demons. As our own powers increase, there will surely be a corresponding decrease in humankind's tendency to seek answers and solace in religion or superstition. For example, Nature or the gods take thousands or millions of years to accomplish the slow process of evolutionary change. Modern technology can, in an instant, reproduce all the information of recorded history. With advances in nanotechnology we may some day be able to instantaneously arrange matter into any desired configuration.

Reengineering of genetic code may enable us to reduce or eliminate genetic disease and defects, perhaps even reproduce organs, bones, or tissue that is less likely to fail or be subject to disease.

Our relationship to the space-time continuum could also be modified. For example, we may be able to travel through time and space without the need for interstellar transport systems, to project human intelligence almost anywhere in the universe — in other words, unknowingly we are evolving toward a reinvention of our gods. We may even, in the future, find that we have outgrown them.

To those who might feel threatened by such concepts, it is not intelligence that we must fear, but ignorance.

IN CONCLUSION

We have arrived at a time when mathematical logic and computers can assist us in unraveling many of the processes of human thought, our growing understanding of which will enable us to enhance future computer technology. Our existing economic and political structures and processes no longer provide the support needed to keep up with and implement changes in technology. Their focus on profit, secrecy, and competition runs counter to the possibilities for positive change afforded by the current, democratic broadening of technology, for instance the Internet with its spirit of collaboration and open exchange of information. It is time to explore new social and economic structures.

In time, the computer and social cybernation may be thought of as the only means of social management that are entirely free of selfish motivation. This may be the most humane approach to our human dilemmas.

We require a global perspective, international cooperation and planetary planning in terms of available resources. This planning must directly relate to the carrying capacity of the earth to meet the needs of all people. This can best be accomplished by using a constantly updated, computerized model of our planetary resources in a resource-based economy.

Advanced social systems do not require scientists or governments to tell them how to operate. The ultimate decision-making authority represents the expression of all humankind. This applied vision of science can serve the common good, a goal that has eluded human civilization for centuries. Although this revolution is still largely in the future, the possibility of a better life for all the inhabitants of our planet will depend, ultimately, on the choices we make today.

ROBOTS CONSTRUCTING ROBOTS

These "multi access industrial robots" utilize vast information resources, which enable them to receive commands via satellite up-link or on-site. They can also be designed to take appropriate actions in the absence of human directives by combining an array of Micro Electro Mechanical Systems (MEMS) and sensors and receivers with sophisticated decision-making circuits and artificial intelligence programs. They will be capable of handling a wide range of industrial production tasks, and will even be able to upgrade their level of service and replace their own parts. When necessary, these mega robots will communicate with one another and coordinate the logistics and delivery of the required materials for each project.

NANOTECHNOLOGY

The future of nanotechnology offers enormous potential. Nanotechnology combines optics and lasers, and will eventually enable us to assemble matter, atom by atom, into whatever molecular structure is needed. Nanotechnology will lead to a sub-microscopic revolution in all fields, including the way in which we conduct human affairs.

MEGA-EXCAVATION MACHINES

This scene depicts a laser excavator of the future. Such devices, directed via satellite, would be capable of fusing the earth beneath it into a molten, magma-like material, thus contouring the earth to aid in the construction of canals, roads, and waterways.

AUTOMATED TUNNEL ASSEMBLING MACHINE

Tunnel segments float down canals by the use of very large flotation devices. This automated tunnel-assembling machine lifts the prefabricated segments and places them in their required positions. Once completed, the tunnels are used for high-speed, mag-lev transportation.

THE CONSTRUCTION OF TOWERS

These towers are designed specifically for regions where earthquakes are prevalent. Such cable-suspended structures easily withstand a wide range of movement, stresses, and strains. Circular towers radially arranged in a city design may be self-erected efficiently and rapidly around a central core that houses elevators and all other household utilities. The translucent windows serve as photovoltaic generators, and the intensity of the light entering the windows can be varied electronically. All window cleaning and maintenance is automated.

MASSIVE LIFTING CRANE

This multi-function crane is designed to lift freeform structures and position them on foundations and stilts or transfer them to vertical lift systems that place the units on towers. Upon completion of their task, these self-erecting cranes can be automatically disassembled into a compact form for easy transportation to the next assignment.

MASS-PRODUCED EXTRUDED DWELLINGS

This demonstrates how lightweight, carbon fiber-reinforced, concrete apartment dwellings could be produced as continuous extrusions, then separated and positioned in place by the mega machine below. The outer shells of these efficient structures serve as photovoltaic generators.

LIFT AND POSITIONING CRANE

This automated machine places these prefabricated dwellings on site where they can be positioned in place by the machine shown on the adjacent page. It is designed to handle structures of many different configurations.

MEGA MACHINES

The machine in the foreground is a multi-function unit. As shown, it lifts and inserts pre-fabricated housing components into a support structure. Although these "prefab" units will be composed of standard components, they will be of a modular design of such diverse array as to allow maximum individual expression in interior design and décor.

AUTOMATED CONSTRUCTION SYSTEMS

The construction of these industrial and research complexes can be carried out by robotic equipment that receives instructions via satellite. These construction crews of the future consist of automated cranes that travel along the buildings' length, installing floors, windows, curtain-walls, roofing, and other components from the ground up, entirely free from human intervention. These devices will contain self-monitoring sensors to minimize industrial accidents or collisions with other devices or living beings.

CHAPTER 9

WHEN GOVERNMENT BECOMES OBSOLETE

GOVERNMENTS TEND TO ENACT many different kinds of laws in an attempt to control society. However, we find no evidence of a deliberate plan by any government to design a sustainable and workable social system to uplift the lives of everyone rather than those holding high positions in the established order.

Visionaries have sought to improve the lives of people by instigating changes within the established social order. The Semanticists called for improvements and clarifications of meaning in our language. The Communists advocated state-ownership and the end of capitalism and human exploitation. The Fascists created a dictatorship of the rich and powerful. Socialists called for a re-ordering of our priorities to serve humanity by a more equitable distribution of existing resources. Religious groups crusade for a return to simpler times, to family values and the teachings of their charismatic leaders. We call for the establishment of scientific scales of performance applied to the social system for the benefit of all people.

With the application of the methods of science to the social system people would have a better understanding of nature and the symbiotic process of which we are an integral part. This could help to provide an understanding of the interrelationship between ourselves and nature and prevent the over-exploitation of the land and sea.

Many people believe that government leaders bring about change with a deep concern for the well-being of their citizenry. Nothing could be further from the truth. Nor did past shifts in society come about as the results of changes in the schools or the home. All established government systems tend to preserve and uphold their own interests and power-base.

The real forces responsible for change have more to do with unforeseen, external events or biosocial pressures that physically alter our environment and established social arrangements: for example, the infusion of machines and processes that replace people and remove their means of making a living, adverse natural conditions of drought, flood, storm, and earthquake, manmade disasters of economic oscillations, or some outside threat of hostile nations.

The industrial revolution did more than move the centers of population from small farms to large cities. It changed how we relate to our communities. World War II changed the accepted roles of women in this country. Vast droughts and wars in Africa today are moving whole populations from their ancestral, tribal lands into the cities, destroying entire cultures almost overnight.

Laws are, at best, attempts to placate or control a population. They work only sporadically.

Another effective method designed to control human behavior is the use of early indoctrination towards a given set of values, sometimes manifesting itself as patriotism, propaganda in the national interest, or outright nationalism. In this way, most of the citizenry will tend to support an existing government, while unaware that other options are available.

Yet another safeguard enacted by the politicians is the perpetuation of the concept of responsibility, that we are all in effect responsible for our own shortcomings, failures, and misfortune, when in fact — in accordance with natural laws that govern all activities on Earth — most of our actions are determined by the circumstances that surround us. Many of our so-called free choices have been greatly influenced by the culture and the surrounding values of our times.

All manmade laws are developed to preserve the established order and to protect people from one another in instances such as deceptive business practices, false advertising, theft, and crimes of violence. This calls for constant monitoring of the populace, yet even so the laws are continuously violated. Such problems are largely generated by social insufficiency, not always by the fault of individuals. People cry out for laws for the relief of hunger, poverty, war, oppression and scarcity, but the answer must lie in removing the conditions that are responsible for these problems. There is so much economic deprivation and insecurity — even in the most affluent nations — that no matter the number of laws enacted, the problems persist. Even the legislators who design our laws have permitted gross violations, in some cases breaking the law themselves.

The need for human rights is a result of a scarcity-oriented society. This may be seen with such elements as air and water. Although both are precious necessities to our well-being and survival, there are very few laws regulating how many breaths are taken per hour, because we have such abundance at this time. No-one monitors a gushing spring to see how much water someone takes from it, although fresh water is absolutely necessary for the support of life. If it is abundant, no-one monitors it. In the western US, however, a tangle of laws conflict and overlap on matters to do with agricultural and fishing rights to fresh water.

When a nation creates a set of laws to legislate human behavior, the vast majority of legislators are unaware of the fundamental factors responsible for the need in the first place. All of nature is subservient to natural law. Natural law cannot be violated without serious consequences to the individual, or to societies. Natural laws dominate all living systems. For example, without water, sun, or nutrients, plants and animals would die. In an environment of scarcity, hunger, and poverty, human behavior will adapt itself accordingly.

Where the laws do not correspond to the nature of the physical environment, they will be violated. Look at the myriad of moral codes that attempt to suppress biological sex drives. Eventually, with a deeper understanding of natural law and the effects of social and cultural influences on human behavior, we may begin addressing the real problems rather than punishing those who transgress.

In a resource-based economy social responsibility would not be instilled by force, intimidation, or promises of heaven or threats of hell. Protection of the natural environment would not be a matter of fines or penalties for polluters. Safeguards against abuse could be designed into the environment. A simple example of this may be seen in the proposed design of the cities of the future where people have free access to resources without debt. This would eliminate the need for theft. Such measures are clearly not a matter of passing and enforcing laws to prevent and punish abuse. Rather, they are a means for designing the flaws out of any social venture, thus eliminating the need for many laws.

Paper proclamations carry very little weight in the real world. All such attempts at social order are BS, Bad Science. Not long ago black Americans did not have access to public water fountains, although there existed so-called constitutional guarantees. Any number of similar examples may be cited of the violation of so-called preferred rights.

A society with human concern "designs out" the need for laws and proclamations, by making all things available to all people, regardless of race, color or creed. When governments make laws, we are led to believe that these laws are made to enhance people's lives. In truth, laws are byproducts of insufficiency.

With an increase in population in excess of available resources, values and behaviors change. With scarce resources, management and allocation become stringent. A set of laws evolve which correspond to these changed conditions. Tracking a culture's evolution reveals the events and environmental influences that determined its values, habits, outlooks, beliefs, and social conduct. For example, if an outbreak of disease reduced the male population by 80%, laws regarding sexual behavior and marriage would undergo vast changes.

We long to be free of flawed, corrupted human thinking and emotions, which have made a graveyard of half of the world — in spite of all the laws, paper proclamations and religious teachings intended to preserve and promote the democratic process in all areas of our monetary-based world economy. Even the United Nations, our most enlightened organization, is motivated to a large extent by self- and national-interests, rather than by the overall good of humankind.

As we begin the transition to a fully cybernated process of governing human affairs, newer technologies will be installed that remove human error from the political bureaucracy. These machines could provide the governing bodies with information rather than opinion, thus considerably reducing the influence of bias and irrational or purely emotional elements in the overall management of human affairs. In an emergent, developing social arrangement not yet established, the rules of human conduct will undergo drastic alterations and changes.

A world-based resource economy could bring about vast changes in human and interpersonal relations, without the enactment of laws. It could introduce a set of values relevant to the needs of all people. A world-based resource economy utilizes all of the world's resources and technical information as the common heritage of all nations, for the benefit of all. This is the unifying imperative. Once installed, the world could witness an end to the need for armaments, war, drugs, greed, and all of the other problems brought about by the endless pursuit of money and power.

Humans require an education system that teaches process and analytical skills rather than incoherent facts. Dialogue would replace debate. Semantics would be a core skill to greatly improve human communication. Students would intelligently evaluate a situation and access relevant information rather than solve stock problems. It is not that they suddenly become better or more ethical, but that the conditions responsible for hostile and ego-centric behavior are no longer present.

Today we try to control human behavior by enacting laws or signing treaties without changing the physical conditions responsible for aberrant behavior. When the earth's resources become the common heritage of all people the necessity for these irrelevant laws and social contracts vanish.

As for "who" will govern, the more appropriate question is "how will people be governed?" People do not have to be governed or require leaders unless they are ignorant, captive, wage slaves, or agree to be subjected to a dictator. If the free enterprise system does not include job security, medical care, and all the other necessities that secure the position of the population as a whole, a wide range of conflicts and unmanageable human behaviors results, no matter how many laws are passed.

No "one" will decide who gets what. Perhaps the closest analogy within our present culture would be the public library, in which anyone has access to any book of his or her choice. Goods and services could be made available in a similar manner across the entire spectrum of the social system. Unfortunately, we are in the habit of thinking that someone has to make the decisions regarding our needs. This would not be the case in the operation of a cybernated, resource-based society.

In the near future, due to such advances in technology as artificial intelligence, cybernation, and nanotechnology, we could achieve a global community and a common vision for humanity. Computerized technology will have greater success uniting people and eliminating scarcity than have all of the world's religions and democratic ideals combined. We can now transcend the limitations of a monetary system, and in time may outgrow our need for politicians and artificial, manmade laws intended to preserve and perpetuate the status quo. *AI* could regulate production, transportation, and all burdensome and monotonous tasks — *but not people.* A highly integrated complex of computers that serves, *but never enslaves,* humankind could carry out the major tasks of decision-making and environmental management.

I must again emphasize that this approach to global governance has nothing whatever in common with the present aims of an elite to form a world government with themselves at the helm, and the vast majority of the world's population subservient to them. This newer vision of globalization empowers each and every person on the planet to be all that they can be, not to live in abject subjugation to a corporate governing body.

The question is, can we grow beyond thinking that "someone" has to make our decisions for us?

CHAPTER 10

WHO WILL MAKE THE DECISIONS

THROUGHOUT HISTORY, the societal decision-making process has gone though a number of changes. At one time, primitive tribes and their ruling chieftains and kings decided upon a set of laws, beliefs, and mores designed to support and defend the ruling oligarchies. As primitive cultures joined together, possibly for mutual protection, the chieftains of the various tribes shared some decision-making.

With the advent of nations, councils were appointed to participate in decision-making, to prevent any one of the leaders from dominating. However, the less privileged were not included in this process. As the ruling classes imposed greater hardships on their subjects through taxation and other abuses of power, uprisings by the oppressed people, intrigue, sabotage, and assassinations forced changes in the laws of the land. Governing bodies were then appointed to carry out and uphold laws.

Although wealth has always "bought" political offices, it was not until the beginning of the nineteenth century that financial interests began in earnest to play a leading role in inappropriate decision-making. Many politicians will use every legal means of deception known to consolidate their position, in the process repeating old slogans that have been used for centuries — "a return to family values," "to serve God and country," and other verbal expressions of undefined goals. They talk around every significant issue without saying anything of content, placing a great deal of emphasis on the role of law and order in government and on international agreements. They enact new laws to try to control the behavior of people and if these don't work, they resort to a tried-and-true method — the use of force, of boycotts and blockades. But none of the methods used seems ever to address the root cause.

Most people still believe that all that is needed to set things right is to replace the incompetent and corrupt officials in government with decent men and women of high moral character. Although we occasionally find politicians of sincere intent, they too are usually unable to find answers to the problems that exist at any given point in time. Human systems fail, obviously, to serve the needs of humanity. This is true across the entire span of human administration: the church, the government, the military, and the banks. In times past, most of the social designs were unsuccessful for the majority of people because their designers were unable to transcend the limits of their own environmental conditioning. We tend to bring our past into the present and project it into the future.

Today, the laws that govern our society are not based on any truly comprehensive studies. They are based on opinions and traditional practices. For example, our current approach to dealing with an increase in crime is to build more prisons rather than to alter the conditions responsible for socially offensive behavior. In a recent discussion with criminologists, it was pointed out that if our crime rate continues at its current level, more than half the US population will be in prison by the year 2010. The other half may well have to guard them. Rather than depend on a failed system of punishment or incarceration after the damage has been done, a more effective approach to solving our problems would be to shift our attention to the scourges of poverty, malnutrition, poor role models, violence in the media, and stresses in family life, while making more of an effort to teach people how to resolve conflict without the use of physical force.

The discovery of scientific principles enables us to validate and test many proposals. If someone claims that a particular structural element can support a specific number of pounds per square inch, this hypothesis can be tested and either substantiated or negated based upon the test results. It is precisely this process of testing which enables us to design and construct bridges, buildings, ships, aircraft, and all other mechanical wonders.

In the new social design as outlined in this book, scientific and analytical principles can be applied not only to industry and construction, but also to all of the personal components of society. This may eventually lead to the application of more scientific resources to the study of human behavior. The most difficult aspect of the redesign of a culture is the seemingly undemocratic approach to the problem. By what authority does any group presume to impose an arrangement of social affairs on others who may be living in the arrangement?

This brings up three questions of primary importance to the redesign of a culture:

1. For whom is the culture designed?
2. What ends is it designed to serve?
3. Who will benefit, the rulers or the ruled?

Thought history, social affairs have either been pre-arranged, or have eventually worked out to benefit the power elite and money interests. Even in so-called democracies this has been the case. People fear a planned social system may not serve their interests. They perceive a very real danger that the introduction of any new social arrangement carries with it the possibility of the development of a new elite.

If a particular religious group were to design a society, it would quite naturally reflect the group's belief's — the "will of the people". The majority of this group would democratically agree that theirs is a good social design. The atheist, agnostic, Hindu, Muslim, and all others not represented would naturally object. What is really needed is a system to determine the most appropriate direction that will be agreeable to all. As difficult as this may appear, it can be done.

Today we have a decentralized system of decision-making, and the decision-makers are seldom aware of problems in regions outside their immediate vicinity. Those of us in sub-tropical Florida have difficulty understanding water rights in Arizona. A Berger of Morocco would be challenged to design a health plan that matched the life styles of people in Norway. Each of us must participate. And we need verifiable and recent information on which to plan.

When computers eventually have their electrical sensors extended into all areas of the social complex, we will be able to return to the centralization of decision-making. In a global resource-based economy the decisions would not be based on local politics but on a holistic problem solving approach. The earth itself, and all the life on it, must be seen as constituting a single system.

This centralized system could be connected to research labs and universities, so that all data is monitored and updated constantly. Most of the technology to allow such infrastructure management is currently available.

For example, when the electrical sensors are extended into the agricultural region, these computerized systems would be able to manage and control all of the agricultural requirements by monitoring the water table, insects, pests, plant diseases, soil nutrients, and so forth.

Computers and artificial intelligence will serve as the catalyst for change. They will be able to establish scientific scales of performance. It is doubtful that in the latter part of the twenty-first century people will play any significant role in decision-making. Eventually the installation of *AI* and machine decision-making will manage all resources serving the common good.

Computers as decision-makers will always scan for new information and methods of conserving resources to coincide with the carrying capacity of each geographical region. This will result in a more humane and meaningful approach for shaping tomorrow's civilization, one that is not based on the opinions or desires of a particular sect or individual.

In the event of a breakdown or regional or national emergency, the special information and already-developed alternative plans for any of the known types of catastrophes that occur would be available, just as military contingency planning is done today.

All decisions would be made on the basis of a comprehensive resource survey and the availability of energy or existing technology — not on the advantage to be gained by any nation or select group of people. This resource survey would coincide with the carrying capacity of each geographical region of the global environment

CHAPTER 11

CLEAN SOURCES OF ENERGY

Some will claim that limited resources prevent us from achieving a society of abundance. This is simply not so. We still have more than enough resources to achieve a high standard of living for everyone. But it's time to move beyond our failed programs and frustrations to innovative solutions that could be readily applied if we were to direct our attention to overcoming scarcity. We have the capability to intelligently apply the humane use of science and new technology to provide for most human needs, and to reclaim and restore the natural environment.

Fossil fuels such as oil and coal allowed our civilization to progress to its present state of development. However, these energy sources are also limited and non-renewable resources, and one of the many environmental dangers.

In the process of designing a new civilization we must harness energy, a major source of the material well-being for all nations. This is a double-edged sword. When placed in the hands of private interest and greed, energy can be used for destruction. The current stock of atomic weapons can destroy the world many times over. But fusion power and other forms of clean sources of energy, when applied intelligently with emphasis on human and environmental concern, could provide all of the nations of the world with clean, unlimited energy sources and a standard of living unattainable today.

Much remains to be accomplished in the undeveloped areas of our planet. Vast and untapped energy sources remain largely unexplored and untouched; amongst these are wind, wave and tidal action, ocean currents, deep ocean pressure and temperature differentials, falling water, geothermal and electrostatic power, hydrogen and natural gas, algae, bacteria, phase transformation, and thermionics, or the conversion of heat into electricity by boiling electrons off a hot metal surface and condensing them on a cooler surface. Additionally, there is the untapped potential of Fresnel lenses, inflatable dome versions of which are being developed for use as optical concentrators in solar power systems.

Fusion power welds together light atoms such as hydrogen and lithium. Fusion energy is the same energy that drives the cosmos and the stars. When we learn how to harness it, the world's energy problems can be solved forever, without any detrimental effects or dangerous toxic materials to be disposed of. The only residue would be the clean ash of helium.

Oceanographers tell us that the world's oceans, occupying 70.8% of the earth's surface, possess an endless supply of surging energy called deuterium, a heavy hydrogen atom locked in the seawaters. According to John D. Isaacs and Walter R. Schmitt, the amount of fissionable uranium and thorium in the oceans can support our present level of power production for millions of years. It is highly probable that in the next century our main source of energy will be produced by thermonuclear fusion or geothermal extraction. Both appear relatively free of many of the hazards inherent in energy produced by nuclear fission.

The transfer of electrical energy will probably be facilitated by improved methods of superconductivity, utilizing cryogenics as part of the international power grid. This grid could serve primarily as a supplement or backup to self-generating structures within the cities. A key element of the design of cities in the future will be the embedding of all necessary energy creation within the structure of the city itself.

We could also utilize solar concentrators as an alternative to fossil fuels for the generation of heat. As of this writing, the Argonne National Laboratory and ARDI are developing a production technique for solar cells that will be nearly 70% efficient at a cost one-tenth that of silicone-based cells. There are many other possibilities for developing photovoltaic systems that generate electricity while harnessing the currently untapped radiant heat energy.

The world's most powerful single hydro-electric project is now being constructed in the Tsangbo Bend in Eastern Tibet, where the river Tsangbo is fed by the great glaciers and waterfalls which descend over seven thousand feet. When the Chinese harness the energy of this dam, it is estimated that the turbines in this power project will be capable of producing far greater than forty million horsepower. This is equal to the total world production of hydroelectric power today.

Another vast, untapped energy option is the development of piezoelectric materials. This source could be employed by using laminated systems inside cylinders, activated by the rise and fall of the tides. A recent development of one these materials is polyvinylidene-fluoride. Five square kilometers can supply electricity for two-hundred-and-fifty thousand people at a cost of one to three cents per kilowatt power, a considerable savings over fossil fuels.

If we developed and harnessed only 1% of the geothermal energy that is available in the crust of the earth, all of our energy problems would be eliminated. Geothermal energy can supply us with more than 500 times the energy contained in all the fossil, oil, and gas resources in the world. Geothermal power plants produce very little sulfur, compared to fossil fuels, and emit no nitrogen oxide or carbon dioxide. A relatively small area of land is required for the power plant itself. Geothermal power is the most economical and efficient way to heat and cool buildings. Natural heat stored underground in combination with the permafrost zones could generate thermal electric power and utilize this power to cool buildings in warm weather by means of geothermal heat pumps.

Geothermal energy can also be used to grow plants year round in enclosed areas, as has already been accomplished in Iceland and other areas. In this way an enormous amount of fresh vegetables could be cultivated in all seasons. A similar process could be used for fish farming and all other regions where heating and cooling is needed. If we had applied just one tenth of what we've spent on military equipment to the development of geothermal generators, we could have long ago solved any energy shortages.

In our resource-based economy, a comprehensive analysis of the environmental, human, and social impact would be carefully analyzed before construction on any project. In all endeavors, the major concern would be to protect and restore the environment for the benefit of all living creatures in the community of life. Of course, the purpose of the construction and development of these power projects is also to free human beings from unnecessary expenditure of energy and from laborious tasks. Up to the present, social development in our monetary oriented society evolved in a haphazard manner, affected by many interacting variables. This process only retarded the advantages inherent in a global cooperative project to develop renewable energy resources rather than exhaust limited resources.

At present we have the means to determine globally the best energy resources available for each geographical location on our planet. What is desperately needed in this world of high technology and rapid change is an energy development strategy on a global scale. To develop a global, sustainable strategy would call for a joint venture of international planning on a level never before achieved.

Eventually international life arteries could serve all nations economically and efficiently. Only by utilizing the best planetary planning can wasteful consumption be reduced considerably. And it is only by reducing wasteful consumption that we can achieve our end goal, that of the highest possible standard of living for all of the world's peoples.

HARNESSING THE GULF STREAM

These underwater structures convert a portion of the flow of the Gulf Stream through turbines to generate clean electric power. The turbines would have a centrifugal separator and deflectors to prevent harm to marine life.

BERING STRAIT DAM

A major development in the future could be the construction of a land bridge or tunnel across the Bering Strait. The primary function of this span would be to generate electrical power and house facilities for collecting and processing marine products. Beneath and above the ocean surface would be tunnels to transport passengers and materials. Pipelines to conduct fresh water from melting icebergs to other parts of the world may also be incorporated. Not only could this structure provide a physical link between Asia and North America, it could also serve as an avenue for social and cultural exchange.

DESALINIZATION PLANT

This mega-machine transports a transparent enclosure used for evaporative condensation. It would be placed over canals, some of them containing salt water, and could serve as a desalinization plant to supply clean water for drinking, irrigation, and other needs. This is accomplished by harnessing the power of the sun and will eliminate water shortages throughout the world.

GEOTHERMAL ENERGY PLANTS

In the future, as refinements in conversion technologies increase its feasibility, geothermal energy will take a more prominent role in reducing the threat of global warming. Readily available in many regions throughout the world, this source alone could provide enough clean energy for the next thousand years.

CHAPTER 12

CHANGING HUMAN NATURE

MUCH OF THE BEHAVIOR ACCEPTABLE TODAY would be socially offensive in a saner or more logical social arrangement. But whatever values, ideals, and behavior people aspire to cannot be fully realized when there is hunger, unemployment, deprivation, war, and poverty. People deprived of their income will often do whatever is necessary to provide the necessities of life for themselves and their families. Their values may be exemplary, but their behavior will reflect the reality of the situation. After World War II, for example, even the most respectable German families could be seen fighting over scraps of food in garbage cans to survive. In a scarcity-oriented society generosity is often a rare occurrence.

It is not enough to design new cities and make sweeping generalizations about human participation and democratic ideals. We must reexamine our dominant values and how and why they evolved.

During the transition to this saner world, there will still be a great deal of interpersonal conflict, egocentric behavior, and all of the other problems that plague our present day monetary society. Therefore it is essential that we utilize newer methods of evaluation to greatly enhance human behavior.

When we examine human behavior in the same manner as any other physical phenomenon, we will be more capable of understanding the physical factors that are responsible for shaping our values and behavior. In the natural sciences all physical phenomena are acted upon by resident forces. For example, a sailboat does not sail of its own accord; rather, it is activated by the wind. A telephone pole does not just fall to the ground; it is acted upon by rain, gravity, wind and a number of other variables.

Human behavior in all areas is just as subject to natural laws and the actions of external forces: it is generated by the many interacting variables in one's environment. This applies even to behavior that is socially offensive. It is often influenced either by one's experiential back-ground, nutritional factors in early life, or a number of other interrelated environmental factors. When one sees a dog leading a blind person across the street we tend to think it is a good dog. But when we see a dog behave offensively we call it a bad dog. The dog is neither good nor bad. A dog can be trained to be ferocious or to help the blind. Both animals could be of the same breed, even from the same litter. Their behavior is due to the differences in training.

To put it another way, try to imagine an ancient Roman family watching Christians being fed to lions. Someone of today might be horrified and believe the people watching had trouble sleeping that evening. But they most likely had no trouble sleeping at all. Such bloodshed was the cultural sport of the times. Lion and Christian were looked upon with equal disdain.

Or imagine a modern day fighter pilot, trained in warfare and taught a similar disregard for the other's culture and beliefs, losing sleep over the fact that he shot down twenty planes and burned several inhabited villages. More likely, he will beam as he is presented a medal, and adorn his aircraft with symbols of his "kills." The pilot reflects the values of his culture just as the Roman family does. What we call our 'conscience' and 'morality' are not determined by an invisible "higher self". They are largely determined by geography, the times, and the individual's upbringing.

One of the greatest limiting factors in human systems is our inability to grasp the significance of resident forces and the extent to which that environment shapes our thinking, values, and/or behavior. When we speak of environment we mean all of the interacting variables, which are the prime contributors of our mindset.

A fundamental consideration in the physical sciences is that one must attempt to identify all of the physical factors responsible for certain outcomes. For example, when an automobile acts in an unusual way most mechanics can account for the reasons and identify the physical factors for that condition. When a human being appears at a hospital with a certain kind of injury, even if he or she is unconscious and unable to identify the cause of the injury a competent medical staff can usually identify the probable cause.

With certain forms of aberrant behavior neurologists, biochemists and psychiatrists can, to a limited extent, identify some of the conditions responsible for this behavior. Even in everyday life, evidence supports the connectivity of influential events all around us. But we often fail to apply the same methods of evaluation that are used in the physical sciences to human behavior.

In many instances our collective values are influenced by an existing social structure or sub-culture within society. For ill or well, social systems generally tend to perpetuate themselves and all of their strengths and shortcomings. In our era of mass-communication, the media-controllers and established institutions influence the national "agenda," which in turn influences much of our behavior, expectations and values.

Whether they realize it or not, most people are constantly manipulated through the media. If you doubt this, check your public TV station for an international news broadcast. Comparing that newscast to you regular newscast could easily lead you to think that the reporting originated from different planets. One must watch with great skepticism.

Our most cherished beliefs are influenced by books, motion pictures, television, religions, role models and the environment we live in. Even our notions of good and evil and our concepts of morality are part of our cultural heritage and experiences. This method of control does not require the use of physical force and has been so successful that we no longer recognize or feel the manipulation.

The dominant values of any social system rarely come from the people. Rather, they represent the views of the dominant control group — the church, the military, the banks, the power elite or any combination of these — which determines the public agenda, the courts, taxes, etc., all of which serve their own interests and perpetuate the illusion that society's values are determined from the ground up. And governments suppress or explain away any deviations that may threaten them.

The fear of retribution from gods and demons is still effective at controlling ignorant and superstitious populations in both developed and undeveloped nations. There are many who actually believe that demons are responsible for anti-social behavior, and that they can be cast out by rituals and incantations. Accordingly, they are unable to evaluate the effects that environment and experiences have upon their behavior. Many people still believe that volcanic eruptions, thunder and lightning, and all manner of cataclysms are manifestations of anger by gods or demons, and that inanimate objects have their own will and act on their own accord.

All human beings are subject to the influences of their surrounding environment. These influences become so ingrained in our habits, thoughts, feelings, and outlooks that we actually believe learned behavior is part of human nature. Even those individuals that feel they are making their own decisions, despite their cultural indoctrination, have been influenced by their surroundings. This is why we fail to critically examine our values and beliefs, and still adhere to myths, superstitions, and outdated customs which have little or no relationship to our survival.

The control of nations and individuals has not been easy because we have such little understanding about ourselves and the conditions that are responsible for shaping our behavior. People know less about their own behavior than they do about the physical world around them. That is why the dominant systems of man-made laws, and the use or threat of force have been frequently used. This technique has been tedious in its application and uncertain in its outcome. Today most of us perpetuate these conditions that may have served in earlier times but have little relevance today. What is needed is an intense research program to identify specific conditions and how those conditions influence human behavior: conditions such as environment, nutritional deficiencies, family relationships, violent-media saturation and — to a limited extent — genetic makeup.

The reason a science of human behavior has not been more widely developed is because the focus has been mostly on people and less on identifying the environmental conditions at work on the individual. The belief that our efforts should be concentrated on the development of the individual alone is fallacious. You cannot identify the factors responsible for behavior through the study of individuals, but rather through study of the cultures in which individuals are nurtured. For instance, the differences between a Native American, a thief and a banker are not found in their genes, but instead closely parallel the environment in which they were raised.

Too many people today use genes as a scapegoat for many forms of aberrant behavior, when the major influences have been shown to be environmental. Genetic make-up alone cannot fully explain or illuminate human behavior, the science of which is a clear, if sometimes complex, algorithm of genes, environmental conditions (food, shelter, family dynamics, education, religious training, personal experiences) and the interpretation and decisions each person makes about the world and their place in it, based on these factors.

Our language causes most of our ignorance of natural law. We speak of the sun rising and setting, rather than of the earth's rotation. We talk about plants growing, inferring that this growth is of its own accord, and ignoring the relationship of growth to water, soil conditions and sunlight. When we use terms like "that rock is rolling down the hill," it implies that the rock has free will. *Nothing we have ever observed in the physical world is self-activating.* All the processes in nature are interactive. A stone does not simply roll down an inclined plane; or rivers do not simply flow. Gravity acts upon them. All living and non-living systems are acted upon by resident forces.

In like manner, the same laws that govern nature apply to human beings and are prime factors in shaping values. All human beings are immersed in an environment with an established system of values. It is the major and minor differences within that environment — and to a lesser extent the genetic attributes of the person — that are responsible for the uniqueness of the individual. If the conditions that establish those values remain unaltered, in spite of the urgings of priests, politicians, or poets, the values persist.

Perhaps in the future, if we arrive at a saner culture, people will view our notions of criminal behavior as being naive. In its very basic definition, crime is the taking of something from another without their consent. As Mark Twain once said, there is probably not an acre of land on earth that belongs to its rightful owner. Our ancestors stole the land from older peoples who took the land from others. In that sense, we are all criminals — or have at least benefited from criminal behavior.

Most man-made laws in our present culture are contrived in an attempt to control the behavior and values that serve the vested interests. If we are to reduce the crime rate, we must alter the environmental factors responsible for this socially offensive behavior. And we have to be clear about the behavior. Criminal behavior — like beauty — is often in the eye of the beholder.

In some instances crime comes about when a group of people becomes the victim of insufficient purchasing power, do not identify with the direction of society, or have little knowledge of the consequences of their actions to themselves or to the environment. In regions on earth where there is low population density and an abundance of food and water, there is no need to steal and consequently no laws against it. If the population exceeds the resources of the land then what we call criminal behavior arises as a result of scarcity, whether artificial or real. A psychiatrist once said that if he could open a drawer and give each of his patients $200,000., 85% of his clients would have no need to see him anymore.

Today, our efforts to deal with socially offensive behavior are inadequate and inappropriate. *Eventually it will be realized and understood that most forms of so-called criminal behavior, which will fill the jails well into the twenty-first century, have been generated by the scramble for money and property in an age of often-contrived scarcity and planned obsolescence.* Four out of five of the prison population in the state of New York come from seven of the lowest income areas in that state.

Bigotry, racism, nationalism, jealousy, superstition, greed, and self-centered behavior are all learned patterns of behavior, which are strengthened or reinforced by our upbringing. These patterns of behavior are not inherited human traits or "human nature" as most people have been taught to believe. If the environment remains unaltered, similar behavior will reoccur. When we come into the world we arrive with a clean slate as far as our relationships with others are concerned.

In the final analysis, any judgment regarding undesirable human behavior serves no purpose without an attempt to alter the environment that creates it. In a society that provides for most human needs, constructive behavior would be reinforced, and people who have difficulty interacting in the community would be helped rather than imprisoned.

Aspiring to a particular ethical behavior has to do with human aspirations and ideals. *Functional morality* is the ability to provide a process level to achieve a sustainable environment for all people. By this, we mean providing clean air and water, goods and services, and a healthy and innovative environment that is emotionally and intellectually fulfilling. It is difficult to conceive of any solutions that would serve the interest of the majority in a monetary-based system. None of this can be accomplished without a comprehensive redesign of our social system and eventual replacement of the monetary system by a resource-based economy.

NATURAL LAW

Whether we realize it or not, every human being — be they criminal or saint — is a law-abiding citizen. That is to say, we are all subject to the natural laws that shape our behavior and values, and it is not possible for human life to exist without being subservient to these natural laws.

Today, however, people believe that they are independent of the laws of nature, and place themselves on a pedestal. They are unaware of their dependence upon natural laws. They build different houses of worship and plead with various interpretations of a deity to alter the laws of nature on their own behalf. They submit appeals for deliverance from such disasters as hurricanes, floods, or droughts. The world's religious leaders and their followers cannot stop outbreaks of the flu or prevent floods or hurricanes by prayer. As long as superstition and ignorance prevail, humanity will fall far short of eradicating war, poverty, and hunger. Only when the human race finally accepts the fact that they are not separate entities in the vast symbiotic process of nature, can we truly say that there is intelligent life on earth.

Some believe that certain laws of nature — for example, the sex urge, a completely natural drive — can actually be changed by acts of Congress, and so laws are enacted against certain kinds of sexual conduct or human behavior. Such people are not swayed by the massive amounts of evidence demonstrating that these behavioral drives do not vanish even with the enactment of such laws. It is not possible to entirely prevent such behavior through legislation if it does not correlate with natural laws and principles.

Natural law is inviolable. For example, a human who does not receive proper nutrition will not enjoy physical well-being, will sicken, and will eventually die. There exist fixed properties of the physical world which no amount of human legislation can change. Natural laws are well-known, yet how many people are forced to violate them because of our social and economic insufficiencies?

With every increase in population, the values and behaviors of cultures change. With scarce resources, management and allocation of them become stringent and sets of laws evolve to correspond to the changed conditions. We must stress again that the values, habits, outlooks, beliefs, and social conduct of a given culture are determined by the environmental influences.

The earth has a built-in recycling system, an arrangement that the human race has to a large extent violated. Our rivers, oceans, and water tables overflow with debris, chemical spills, and the runoff of daily living. Landfills contain mountains of toxic and non-biodegradable trash that will last for centuries. Replenishing the environment is very difficult in a world of unregulated competition. As fast as we recover a river, another oil platform is built in the sea. Just as all technology is engineered to perform a given task, the management of the environment that supports all life also requires an intelligent attempt to manage the output and input systems that must exist in harmony with the natural, symbiotic process.

As nations violate the symbiotic process of nature, we pay for it in the loss of arable land, environmental degradation, pollution of the oceans, territorial disputes and wars. In many instances, international agreements and laws become meaningless and counterproductive if they do not conform to the carrying capacity of the environment.

As we observe the natural world around us, we cannot help but admire the functional design and the aesthetic aspects that are byproducts of function. The ingenious economy of natural evolution has produced shapes, forms, coloration and unique configurations that appropriately conform to the environment that nurtured them.

The same laws that govern the physical world and engineering principles are universal in their application to the humanities. What distinguishes the technical person — the scientist or engineer — from the politician or theologian is that, when confronted with technical breakdowns, the former cannot blame the opposite party or the hand of the almighty. They cannot blame incompetence of the former administration. If they did so, it is unlikely that they would ever be called upon for their services. A chemical engineer cannot avoid his or her responsibility by explaining away corrosion in transfer tubes of chemical elements. He or she is responsible for the selection of the materials used. Scientists have no way of avoiding their responsibility for problems encountered. While some people shun accountability, and justify mistakes by pointing out that to err is human, most scientists and engineers seek to minimize the probability of that error. Prior to the building of a dam or any new physical structure, for example, they conduct a great many studies in order to evaluate and uncover insufficiencies in the planning.

Unfortunately, few students learn good analytical skills. The humanities are not held up to this same scrutiny. They present vague and mystical explanations of physical phenomena. Many explanations are accepted without sufficient information or study of the subjects covered. Mystical explanations cannot serve in the practice of engineering or any other branch of the physical sciences. If we do not have sufficient information, our decisions and conclusions will be inappropriate.

Few liberal arts courses provide a foundation for the intelligent analysis required for rational thinking. What is notoriously lacking in students' education is exposure to the natural sciences and the laws responsible for all natural phenomena. In our redesign of education, we propose that intelligent analysis be a core subject in all school curricula.

It has taken many years to realize that the human being is subject to the same laws of nature that propel the planets, stars, and living and non-living systems. Setting human behavior apart from these laws is arrogant, erroneous, and dangerous.

The development of robots and artificial intelligence serves as an extension of the human body. Although seemingly disconnected from us, the cybernated world serves as an advanced and objective extension of collective thinking, and of how humans relate to one another and the world we inhabit. In fact, all the hand tools of primitive tribes and their language evolved as extensions of human attributes. This same process of extensionality is expressed in our books, architecture, mathematics and all branches of the physical sciences. This includes living and non-living systems, which are interdependent to the life process that sustains all of us.

Eventually the realization of this encompassing connectivity between living and non-living systems could enable all of us to outgrow our shallow self-centeredness as a species. This self-centeredness has prevailed within and dominated the human race for untold centuries.

As long as people and their governments remain ignorant of these basic principles, humanity will suffer the consequences. Today the management of human social systems is based upon antiquated concepts and primitive superstitions that serve national interests. We cannot achieve any real progress towards social maturation, no matter how sincere the intent of governments may be, without an understanding of these laws.

The survival of the human race depends on the recognition of these unalterable principles. If we fail to use these principles and continue trying to operate from our anthropocentric pedestal, we will be doomed to repeat the same errors over and over again.

ASSOCIATIVE MEMORY

As we explore human behavior and the influence environment has on people, one question always arises: do we really think? This is a circular question that cannot be answered until we define what we mean by "thinking." Thinking is, at its simplest, talking to oneself. The term thinking evolved as a not-wholly successful means of describing a mental process that was poorly understood at the time. Thinking is influenced by the process called associative memory. Any judgment we make, value system that we uphold, or preferences that we express are always based upon associative memory. It is essentially reflective of the environment and the experiences that we have had.

An example of associative memory would be: if we see a flower somewhat similar to a rose, but with a small, dark spot in the middle, we would probably smell the flower. After all, our experience is that roses smell pleasant. If the odor is instead pungent, the distinguishing black spot would affect our future response with other flowers of similar configuration. We may not shy away from the roses without dark spots, but we will think twice about smelling those we associate with an unpleasant experience.

Associative memory identifies objects, places or people. The same process applies to hearing, touch, smell, feelings, judgments, and opinions. All decision-making systems are based upon associative memory. This is essentially the process by which we formulate our decisions of right, wrong, good, bad, and how we measure aesthetics and beauty. Beauty lies not in the eye, but in the associative memory of the beholder.

To an entomologist the structure of a spider may be appealing, even beautiful, while others may find it repulsive. If we lived in a land where everyone had a nose six inches long, those who did not "measure up" would no doubt have surgery to add to it, to conform to the accepted norms. When an Eskimo not exposed to modern civilization thinks of transportation, it is most likely in the form of a team of dogs pulling a sled. If exposed to no other housing styles, the natives of the Amazon jungle think of a home as a thatched hut. No human being is capable of overcoming the influences of his or her environment; this includes all of one's experiences. Ample examples of this behavior exist in our own culture.

Most of us operate under the assumption that the human brain is a reservoir of limitless, untapped information. People speak of bringing out the best and noblest qualities in humans, but you cannot bring out that which is not there. This notion of the human mind is extremely dangerous and unfounded.

If an electrical engineer of eighty years ago had been handed a microchip and asked to speculate on its use, even if he were to dissect it he would have no basis for interpreting its function. The implications and understanding of associative memory can have a profound effect on the way that we look at the world and ourselves. It may even raise questions as to how much freedom there is in our so-called individuality and freedom of choice.

HUMAN RELATIONS

The greatest lesson we learn may be that when human beings are free of debt, insecurity, and fear of their neighbors they become much more amiable. No one will be out to sell anyone anything or to deprive another of possessions or money. In a resource-based economy, the basis for unhealthy human aggression will be eliminated.

In addition to adequate food, clothing, shelter, heating, energy, health care and education, they must also receive a sense of acceptance, belonging, and self-worth. This new social design proposes just such an environment.

This heightened sociability will come about as we outgrow and remove the conditions that have been responsible for aberrant behavior through the introduction of a more humane and relevant value system. In a non-competitive world, through education and intelligent interaction, people will be lifted out of the mire of shallow self-centeredness that is born of the constant struggle for property, wealth and power.

Once freed of the necessity of meaningless drudgery, debt, money and possessions, people will no longer worry about many of the nagging concerns that consume so much of our attention, such as home mortgages, health care costs, fire insurance, economic recession and depression, and taxes. With the elimination of these burdens and the removal of the conditions that create feelings of envy, greed and competition, our lives would be far more meaningful, more humane and have fewer inconsistencies and conflicts.

HUMAN EMOTIONS

Many human emotions reflect environmental insufficiency, insecurity, and scarcity. Our emotions and how we express them are to a large extent determined by our culture. Here we do not refer to emotions due to physiological reactions such as physical pain, loud noises, or bright lights. By emotions, we mean *patterns of behavior that do not alleviate the problem*. A less scientific but more colorful way of describing emotion in this sense is that it resembles the racing of a car's engine at a stoplight, generating a lot of energy but taking us nowhere.

In fact, a great many human emotions are induced as strategies for achieving self-centered ends such as promotion of nationalism, salesmanship, seduction, flattery, and a myriad other forms of manipulation. They are used to gain control over the actions of others.

When a car skids on wet pavement and crashes, someone may tend to the situation as best he or she can, perhaps holding the injured person's hand until a doctor arrives. We consider such a person to be a caring and concerned individual. Rarely seen or appreciated is the engineer who comes along and adds an anti-skid surface to the pavement, thus eliminating the cause of the accident in the first place. This variety of caring is an emotion translated into a workable solution to eliminate the problem.

A caring society of the future will remove the conditions that are responsible for greed, envy, hate, revenge, and other undesirable human emotions. It will use technology to make certain emotions irrelevant, by getting rid of many of the problems that cause them. In a resource-based economy, when people no longer live in fear of losing their jobs or being insecure in old age, and when they have access to things that were not available to them in a monetary system, then love will not be merely a word, but actually manifested in a way of life. When humans learn to live in harmony with nature and with one another, then spirituality will be a way of life rather than just empty talk. In a more sophisticated and humane society, emotions would be harnessed and expressed by an appropriate behavior or action pattern.

When emotions are translated into a positive, constructive action pattern — when they are used to transcend the limitations of the present culture of war, poverty, and hunger that give rise to so many of these emotions — they will indeed become useful. When they are harnessed in such a way as to transcend the limitations of the present and become expressions of deed rather than simply habitual, unthinking reactions to stimuli, they will serve human beings far better.

Perhaps some day in the future, when there is peace on earth and abundance of resources available to everyone, many of the emotions that have bewildered us for centuries — emotions such as anger, despair, vengefulness, envy, and depression — will begin to abate in power, perhaps even disappear, due to the beneficial effects of our redesigned culture and environment.

CHAPTER 13

TECHNOPHOBIA IN A CYBERNATED AGE

THIS BOOK PROPOSES A PARTNERSHIP between scientific accuracy and imaginative projections, one that may lead to an age in which intelligence is no longer solely associated with human beings. In spite of fears to the contrary, potential problems do not lie between humans and machines, but rather with the limitations of the human intellect in a time of explosive technological development.

Many people fear rapid, technological developments, particularly the automated and cybernated aspects of machines replacing human beings — if not outright, perhaps, then to an extent that would deprive them of their livelihood. Many of these fears have been justified by the rapid increase in production technology requiring considerably fewer workers. This trend seems to be accelerating, and contributes to people's fears of being replaced by superior systems that do not require human participation.

The basic operating concepts of a monetary-based system exacerbate the problem, since profit is of more concern than the individual. Today, machines are not used to enhance the lives of employees by shortening the workday while increasing vacation time and purchasing power. Instead, industries use automation to benefit a select few and the shareholders. In this way the majority of people may very well occupy the role of nonessential personnel that have outlived their usefulness and are set aside, much as obsolete machines are scrapped today. It is not technology that is at fault, but the inhumane use of this technology for private profit. Humans contribute significantly to this misuse of technology by buying stock in and products produced by companies that show little concern for humans or the environment.

A few computer designers today harbor the irrational fear that the machines will eventually dominate people, since their designs are beginning to manifest human attributes. This is the unfounded fear of the technophobe. Machines actually care nothing about whether they turn out five thousand cars a month or five hundred. They merely function as they are designed to. They make no complaints as they toil in the hot sun harvesting crops and planting seeds without rest. They have no sweat glands or physical need for sleep.

It is because they do not have emotions that they will not conspire to enslave human kind. The technophobes, with their unfounded fears that computers and robots will eventually enslave the human race and take over the world, are simply *attributing human characteristics to machines.* They do not posses those human and animal characteristics we call feelings, which are activated by hunger, thirst, sensory stimulation, experience, and internal secretions. When a group of computers are destroyed in the presence of another computer there is no anger, resentment, or lust to "get even" on the part of the surviving computer. Many humans, particularly science fiction writers, project these characteristics into the machines of the future. Even when machines simulate emotions they are not genuine; they do not feel one way or another about any issue.

The fears that machines will increasingly regulate our lives, rob us of our natural instincts and eventually threaten our most cherished values, such as our family and spiritual beliefs, are erroneous. Even though machines may provide us with rapid transportation, prefabricated abundance, and artificial intelligence, people still harbor these fears.

Some individuals distrust a computerized society and the possible failures of the machines. They feel this technology makes us more like machines, driving us towards uniformity, resulting in the loss of individuality and that which we cherish most, freedom of choice and privacy.

In defense of machines, perhaps we would be better off if people behaved more like them. There is no question that some machines are poorly designed, but the flawed natures of human beings in high places surpass, by far, the illusion of the destructiveness of machines.

There is no evidence of machines acting against human beings of their own accord, except in naïve science fiction stories. Humans program machines and direct their use. It is not machines that are to be feared; it is the misuse and misdirection of these machines that threaten humankind. We must not forget that the bombing of cities, the use of nerve gas, prisons, death camps, and torture chambers have all been managed and operated by human beings, not machines. Even atomic weapons and guided missiles are built and directed by people. People pollute the environment — our air, oceans, and rivers. The use and sale of harmful drugs, the distortion of truth, bigotry, and racial hatred are all part of flawed human systems and false indoctrination.

Machines are not the danger: we are. As long as we fail to take responsibility for our relationship to our fellow human beings and the intelligent management of our planetary resources, we remain the greatest danger to our planet. If there would ever be a conflict between men and machines, we can be fairly certain as to who would start it! It is time we acknowledged that while there may be a moral high ground, none of us are currently standing on it. The most powerful testimony to our ignorance comes from the very scapegoats we blame for our social ills: too much technology, foreigners and minorities, "position of the planets," demonic influences, and subjective moral standards. None of these are relevant, they only serve to divert our attention away from the real problems.

Science and technology created none of our problems. Our problems arise from human abuse and misuse of other people, the environment, and technology. Downsizing is not due to machines displacing people. In a more humane civilization such machines would be used to shorten the workday, increase the availability of goods and services, and lengthen vacation time. If we utilized new technology to raise the standard of living for everyone, then the infusion of machine technology would serve to benefit all people.

As the dangerous side effects of the misuse of technology escalate — environmental pollution, the over-exploitation of the land and sea, and the wasted resources of war and unnecessary human suffering — there is a backlash for the return to a simpler life and less technology. At the same time people call for the return to more humane values and a considerable reduction in the rate of technological development.

Those who nostalgically advocate a return to the "simple life" and "going back to the land" are misinformed and limited in their thinking. Try to imagine what would happen if we removed all of the machines in people's homes: the radio, television, computer, telephone, electric light, oven, refrigerator, and heating and cooling system. We do not see such people tossing their machines out of the house or going even one week without the use of their car. These are people who are preoccupied with wishful thinking and irrelevancies. They have always been free to give up their modern conveniences and move into a cave, if they choose to do so. But how far back does one really want to go?

These people are apparently unaware of the high rates of infant mortality, women dying in childbirth, malnutrition, and death due to infectious disease that were prevalent in earlier times. Any such regression or return to the past would be a vast waste of the human potential. Do we not instead require better means of communication, transportation, increased agricultural yield and housing for the billions of people throughout the world?

If those whose voices are raised against technology were able to turn back the clock in the name of some vague, humanitarian values, we would condemn millions of people to a state of permanent misery and unnecessary suffering.

The idea of a hand-tool economy in which humans spend most of their time providing for the bare necessities of life, devoting long hours of toil to digging wells, gathering wood for energy, hand pumping water and washing clothes in the river, leaves little or no room for the development of the individual. This holds true, also, for those in an industrial society seated on a production line who are exposed to a cycle of repetitive motions in the production of parts. We are using a very small portion of the human being in these instances and neglecting the most important aspect of being human, that which is supposed to set us apart form other animal forms — our intellect.

One of the most shameful aspects of the twentieth century is the degree of technological illiteracy affecting millions of people, despite access to the broadest range of knowledge the world has ever assembled. Even in the United States, vast numbers of people go through their day without the least idea of how a grocery scanner or a toilet works. They are only faintly aware of their dependency on dams, power plants, mass transportation, electrification and modern agricultural science for their very existence. When they turn on a light, they give little thought to the centrally controlled power grid that links the widely separated power stations by long distance transmission lines. These lines serve as the productive life force of industry, transportation and the electrification of the society.

Without access to electrical power, the telephone, air conditioning, radio, television, and computers, what we have come to accept as modern society would disappear. Without electricity the gas pump at your favorite station stops. Without refrigeration, preservation and transportation of food on a global scale would be impossible. No hospital could sustain life during surgery without machines that monitor the patient. All the leading nations of the world depend on technology for their very survival. Without modern nutritional facilities, public health would be threatened and our standard of living would be reduced to a hand-tooled economy.

In other words, it is technology that propels today's civilization. Without chemistry, agronomy, engineering, and modern health sciences the world as we know it would not exist. Humanity would be burdened by hard physical labor and longer hours of work just to maintain the bare necessities.

Because many people believe that there is too much emphasis on technology, they fail to see the humane aspects of science. It has actually been called "cold science" — admittedly with some justification in monetary-based societies, in which the tools of science are often directed primarily towards the goals of private profit and the maintaining of positions of advantage.

Many writers and literary people who perpetuate the myth of cold science express technical illiteracy and ignorance of the meaning of science. This may be due to their feeling excluded and wholly unable to grasp the real significance and sensitivity of science.

Some point out the detrimental effects of dams, irrigation canals, and nuclear power projects. They are strangely silent prior to the construction of these projects. In many cases only when the projects fail do the detractors make themselves known — but rarely with a viable solution or alternative. It is not the dams and the power projects that should be cut out; instead it is up to us to devise more effective and practical applications to harness nature and still protect the environment while helping to support human life.

There are always positive effects of all natural phenomena. Whether we view them as good or bad depends on the species affected, and on the effects on human civilization. When a volcano erupts, the dust may be spread over an extensive area, choking out many forms of life; but the lava also provides new soil and fertilization for the growth of new plants. Hurricanes spread seeds in vast areas where they would not otherwise have landed; such "pollination" originally supported the lush growth on many islands. The world of the future will involve harnessing and maximizing the forces of nature and redirecting them in constructive ways that would help support human life, while protecting the natural environment.

It is possible to build dams, canals, and power plants that offer far more than they do today, while minimizing the negative effects. For example, dams can allow for the migration of fish by means of inclined steps that enable fish to ascend to a higher level, or allow for the removal of silt where needed. If we start a project with a full "map" of the proposed plan, not only can we see and prevent damage, but also adjust the design to accommodate the current natural processes — saving time and material. Computer simulation models already exist. Most major projects, however, are undertaken to fit special agendas, primarily business or special interests, and are totally unconcerned with the existing ecology. Much is lost in the process.

Would you trust your life to a machine? Actually, you do so every time you get into an airplane or a car. Chances are you'd much rather come into San Francisco airport in a thick fog while guided by sophisticated electronic instrumentation than by a human pilot who can't see past the nose of the plane! And how many patients in a hospital are kept alive during emergencies by machine life support systems?

As with many other things humans come into contact with, they often tend to personalize the machine. Humans can become emotionally involved with their machines, and even brought to tears or anger over them. Whole groups of people in a motion picture theater watching animated pen and ink drawings identify with the characters and laugh or weep over these nonexistent entities.

People often refer to their automobiles as their "babies". Boats are referred to as "she." Many a husband, when told by his wife or teenager "I've had an accident", inquires first how badly the car was damaged.

Since the advent of the personal computer, machines have become so ingrained in the lives of many people that not only do they depend on the computers to support their livelihoods, but they depend on them to support their mental state as well. In many instances the computers become extensions of themselves and sometimes unknowingly their best friend. Computers never argue or become indignant or jealous, neither do they react to insults. Sitting at a computer keyboard, users indulge their wildest fantasies without having to deal with the hassles of personal contact. The personal computer has become an essential and very extensional part of their lives.

The technological revolution is here to stay and will eventually, whether we support it or not, free people from the never-ending struggle for security. Computers have already invaded our schools, churches, and the highest offices of government, yet they do not intend to enslave or regiment the human race into some form of uniformity. They do not inquire into their users color, creed, sexual orientation, politics, or religion. They are in some respects kinder to us than we are to ourselves.

We need more technology, not less. But we need a new kind of application of technology. If technology were managed intelligently and with human concern, it could be used to overcome scarcity and liberate millions of human beings from the scourges of poverty and social insufficiency.

Rather than consign humanity to eternal slavery to their machines in a monetary wage system, we should allow machines to free human beings from dangerous, boring, or meaningless jobs. Far from being the threat feared by technophobes, machines could be liberators, providing us the time and the resources to help us learn what it really means to be a human being and a member of a world community.

CHAPTER 14

EDUCATION: MINDS IN THE MAKING

THE MORE INTELLIGENT OUR CHILDREN, the better our lives and the richer our culture will be. Today, each and every child using drugs and living a life without direction and purpose is a damaged life we will all have to pay for in the future. It is our children who will inherit the future. With the proper information and nurturing, they will understand the earth to be a fantastic place capable of providing more than enough for the needs of everyone.

The development of a new civilization involves not only the construction of new cities for living, but also the building of positive and caring interpersonal relationships. The young and old of this new civilization will learn to live in harmony with one another. Education plays the most important role in achieving this goal, particularly in children.

The subjects of study will be related to the direction and needs of this new, evolving culture. This new curriculum will emphasize the generalist point of view and the introduction to general science. Students will be made aware of the symbiotic relationships between people, technology, and the environment; they will have a better understanding of the evolution of cultures and the application of advanced technology to this new social design.

Our schools of tomorrow will teach children to be analytical. Students will study the interrelationships of life, rather than discrete and disassociated subject matter. The focus will be on the interrelationships of humans with the earth and with each other. Early education will emphasize understanding and cooperation.

In the redesign of education, the first questions we ask are: what end is education to serve; and in a cybernated world society how do we determine the direction of education? Some goals might be:

1. Working toward the common heritage of all the world's resources.
2. Transcending the need for all of the artificial boundaries that separate people.
3. Replacing the monetary-based economy with a resource-based world economy.

4. Reclaiming and restoring the natural environment to as near natural a condition as possible.

5. Redesigning our cities, transportation systems, and agricultural and industrial plants so that they are energy efficient, clean, and able to conveniently serve the needs of all people.

6. Gradually outgrowing the need for political methods of governance, whether at the local, national, or supranational levels, as a means of social management.

7. Sharing and applying new technologies for the benefit of all.

8. Exploring, developing and using clean, renewable energy sources such as wind, solar, geothermal, and tidal power.

9. Ultimately utilizing the highest quality products for the benefit of the world's people, while eliminating planned obsolescence.

10. Focusing on interpersonal skills that will improve relationships.

11. Requiring an environmental impact study prior to construction of any mega projects.

12. Encouraging the widest range of creativity and incentives toward constructive endeavor.

13. Assisting in stabilizing the world's population through education and voluntary birth control, in order to conform to the carrying capacity of the earth.

14. Eliminating nationalism, bigotry, and prejudice.

15. Phasing out the inclination to any type of elitism, technical or otherwise.

16. Arriving at methodologies through careful research rather than random opinions.

17. Enhancing communication so that our language is more relevant to the physical conditions of the world around us

18. Providing not only the necessities of life, but also offering challenges that stimulate the mind, while emphasizing individuality rather than uniformity.

19. Finally, preparing people intellectually and emotionally for the possible changes that lie ahead.

Ultimately, these goals determine the direction education will take. If we decide to explore the moon's surface or dig a tunnel under the sea, we must first build an organization dedicated to that goal and with the capabilities to accomplish it. To develop a civilization that can provide a higher standard of living for all people and eliminate war, poverty, and hunger, society must adopt goals that can accomplish these ends.

With the impetus of a resource-based economy, this new direction in education would stress a cooperative world enterprise in which individuality, creativity and cooperation could be the norm rather than the exception. It would be free of politics, folkways and superstitions, and encourage the widest possible range of innovative thinking.

In the schools of a unified world civilization, classrooms could provide information about human behavior and the forces that shape our culture and values. All students could have access to information without restrictions of any kind. Individual ideologies would always remain as a set of tools and an associative framework, recognized to undergo self-modification and growth with new information and experiences.

What would likely be perplexing to the citizens of the future is why there was, in the past, only one Edison, one Pasteur, one Alexander Graham Bell, one Tesla and, in general, so few others of their caliber: why was it that so few original minds managed to emerge from the billions populating our planet's history?

Try to imagine a world where thousands of such individuals live and prosper at the same time, thinking and creating to their full ability — a world in which most human beings actively participate in the improvement of the earth's conditions instead of simply toiling to make a living.

At the same time, these people of the future may find it incredible that leaders of independent nations and industries could not grasp the possibilities of a social system of cooperation rather than of competition.

We desperately need a saner mode of civilization that will no longer divide humankind. Residents of new, networked communities would be educated from birth to consider themselves planetary citizens, without sacrificing freedom and individuality to any form of totalitarianism.

SCHOOLS OF TOMORROW

Education will undergo considerable improvements. Children would be given time to explore their own interests while also participating in cooperative behavior and interaction with both other children and the environment, in hands-on experiments and tours of the natural environment, production plants and all related industries.

The learning environment would encourage actual participation on simplified levels. Younger children would plant seeds in soil, irrigate, fertilize them and record their growth, as is presently done in many schools. Actually participating in plant and animal development alters forever a child's view of nature and enhances their comprehension of the way nature works, how all its many and varied functions interrelate with each other. They will come to understand that nature is a symbiotic process and that no single thing enables a plant to grow. They would see that a plant cannot grow without radiant energy from the sun, water, and nutrients, and even the fact that gravity plays a major role in the process.

Children would understand that each individual can take an idea only so far. Others invariably add to it and improve upon it. Each contribution motivates and encourages others. Ideas grow and expand like crystals into varied and complex patterns. With this better realization of our interdependence with one another, self-centeredness gradually disappears.

Patriotism and national pride, which tend to obscure the contributions of other nations, would no longer be relevant to a new, emerging culture. The children could learn, for example, that six hundred years before Christ lived the Arabs developed the electric battery. A thousand years before the Wright brothers launched their first flying machine at Kitty Hawk, the Chinese developed man-carrying kites. A Russian named Tsiolkovsky was first to describe in detail the principals of space flight. A Frenchman, Louis Pasteur, developed an inoculation against rabies. In the sixteenth century, the Italian Leonardo da Vinci envisioned the principals of flight and designed a rudimentary form of helicopter. The Polish astronomer, Nicolaus Copernicus, published his book on the revolution of the celestial bodies. Albert Einstein, a German, gave us the theory of relativity. The contributions of all nations made our standard of living possible and enriched our lives. But we still are only at the threshold of the future.

Students would learn that no single nation has all of the answers nor an answer for all situations. Society is in a constant process of change. Students would understand that there are no final frontiers. They would also realize that each discrete phase of society will evolve a set of values appropriate to that time. All values, including many of the postulates of science, must be utilized as the best tools available at the time. With the advent of additional information and more sophisticated tools, our notion about the nature of the world could be constantly updated. Science would be taught as a set of known facts and applications that would be subject to change as more information becomes available, not as a set of immutable rules and laws.

Children taught through cooperative, participatory, hands-on experiences develop better socialization shills and self-confidence. Rather than rote learning, our new schools provide opportunities for children to improve their interaction with one another in real life situations. In other instances students may choose to explore their independent interests by selecting their own curriculum. If they prefer, they would be assisted by counselors or artificial intelligence machines, which would convey information through words, diagrams, visual displays, and many other methods. Our new schools will accommodate the many, varied ways in which children learn.

Education would emphasize human values and communication, an essential process to improve the interaction and communication between people of all races, color and creeds. Both children and adults can learn to outgrow the self-centeredness that dominates the behavior of many people today. A new form of education could make abundantly clear that our likes and dislikes are based upon our present culture, and that our visions of the future are always culture-bound.

The children would visit the farms, the power plants, the production facilities and the resource centers, and could actually take part in managing and planning their own affairs. Each child could experience leadership by planning activities, and these responsibilities could be constantly rotated so that each student would gain the experience.

If we wish to improve the mental condition of all our children, we must not only educate them through books and other visual aids, but also through games that are both physically and mentally stimulating.

The Children's Centers would be equipped with such books, computers, and a wide variety of visual aids. At these learning centers, the kind of games children play would be relevant to the needs of the child and the emergent culture. Today, far too many of the games available to our children depend on competition and encourage hostility.

The game of chess does not generate creativity in other areas; with practice, strategies for chess may be enhanced but it does not enhance creativity outside of that game. This game takes a tremendous amount of effort to learn but is about nothing in particular. If this same effort was applied to games that improved one's understanding of such areas as nutrition, health, and disease-control, it would be far more beneficial for the player and for society. People consider the chess game a challenge, but its significance is equal to that of a beauty contest. What games will be available in the future?

Consider a game centered on a virtual image of the Earth. As the children touch various areas of the Earth they could learn about the geography and languages of those areas. With laser indicators pinpointing specific areas, they could interact with and receive relevant information about any aspect of the geographical area. This could be done with just as much fun and challenge as are provided by many of the games played today, yet without the need for outsmarting the other players.

Other significant games will translate information about the physical to the needs of the individual and society. There might be games that further one's mathematical abilities. Skeletal structures of humans and other animals, when touched, would verbally identify the structures and organs, teaching anatomy and physiology. The study of plants and all other physical phenomena might be similar.

Further games will encourage creativity. In such an environment of creative games, associative memory and the experience gained form the basis of creative thinking. To think is to make a correlation, and it is the relevance of the correlation that counts. All imagination is based on cumulative experience. The broader the background, the more a person can bring to a subject.

The people of the future would be encouraged to engage in constructive diversity. Even nursery children could participate in games to develop a wide range of flexibility, individual initiative, and creativity, along with a high degree of self-sufficiency. For example, if they were told that 4 and 4 were 8, they would probably reply: "Eight what?" If two drops of fluid are suspended in an acoustical chamber we can by sonic means convert two drops to eight drops, or one drop to four drops. All numerical relationships in the future would be conducted within a given frame of reference.

Today children are not properly taught how to ask questions and examine ideas. Education consists primarily of rote learning, of simply memorizing concepts and propaganda. Children in the future would not be satisfied to accept ideas without an in-depth exploration and understanding of them. If a child of the future were to be told that the country they lived in was the greatest in the world, they might ask "How so?" and "Compared to what set of standards?" The free minds of the twenty-first century would challenge everything — and most would, in fact, be experts at changing their minds.

At an early age children could be exposed to social and cultural anthropology. They could also be exposed to the history of civilization and to the history of technology from bow and arrow to the space age.

Rather than trying to instill in them a sense of self-worth through moral lectures, we could urge children to develop the necessary skills to further their inquiry. Education in the future could be based upon utilizing and harnessing the natural curiosity of children. The children would not, however, get instantaneous fulfillment of their requests. This tends to diminish incentive and makes it almost impossible for them to live without immediate gratification. For example, if a child asked a parent to build a model airplane the parent could say, "I will teach you how to build one". This provides the child with an appreciation for their own accomplishments and improves their self worth. As this process continues over the years the child will develop a higher self-sufficiency and depend less upon others.

Children find animated toys exciting and interesting. In the new schools they could develop their own animated toys. Before they actually build these models, they would be instructed in the use of the necessary crafts. As they develop their skills in working with these tools — while soldering, wiring, bonding, and fabricating — they can actually see and use the results. This would give them an appreciation of the effort that is required to make items they often take for granted. They could constantly learn how to apply high safety standards while working with simple and eventually more complex machines.

At the same time, the students could learn how to design and draw the models they intend to build both by hand and by computer. Science, mathematics, art, written communications, and interpersonal skills come into play in this single task. Once a project is completed, the students will have a better understanding of the relationship between the blueprint and the materials required for completing a project. Mathematics would be taught as part of the design initiative in the building of these projects, so that there is a physical reference for numerical systems. In this more advanced system, it should be an easy task to transfer these principles to all other areas of creativity within the arts and sciences. Through this process, students will be able to grasp the relationships between nature, technology, and civilization.

If we want the children to achieve a positive, constructive relationship with one another and become a contributing member of society, an effective way to accomplish this is by designing an environment that produces that desired behavior. For example, when the children are interested in learning how to assemble a small motor vehicle the design would require four children to lift the car while two others attached the wheels. The rest of the car would be assembled in a similar manner, needing the help and cooperation of everyone to complete the vehicle for their use. This enlightened form of education would help students understand the advantages of cooperation.

Exercise in our school would not be mandatory, monotonous, or involve adversarial competition, but would be incorporated into the classroom experience. A craft shop the children enjoy using might be located on a hilltop in the middle of a lake. To get there the children would have to row a boat or swim, and then climb the hilltop. This not only provides the exercise but also a sense of achievement, which helps their mental health and incentive.

These are simplified examples of complex processes and ideas which should be considered for our redesign of education.

A great deal of attention would be given to emotional development. But perhaps the most important aspect would be on learning to interact effectively with others, share experiences, examine alternative approaches to problems, and allow for cultural and individual differences. This could reduce personal and interpersonal conflicts considerably.

Children will learn to modify their approach to get their point across, employing reason and restraint rather than name-calling or raising their voices. They would learn how to honestly disagree without experiencing bitter feelings. Such judgmental terms as "right" and "wrong" would be avoided and phased out. They would have a much more refined vocabulary and understand such terms as "a closer approximation of reality". Their vocabulary would also be a relevant one, rather than a purely emotional one. A relevant vocabulary will pertain to the situation — for example, "The inclined ramp is too steep for elderly people" — rather than an emotional vocabulary were one might remark, "A moron must have built that ramp." In other words, the child will learn that descriptive and constructive rather than outright criticism may serve to improve the situation.

Education would be participatory. Students would work cooperatively as a team. For example, if a class-group were hiking through a wooded area and came to a stream, one of the children might say to both adults and peers, "I have an idea, and I'd like to hear what you think about it." With this exposure children will have a tendency to listen and ask questions. Rather than being met with phrases such as "that will never work", students and instructors could submit their ideas to the class and test the validity of their proposals, receiving suggestions rather than criticism alone.

These young people would willingly interact with the environment, taking an active role in hiking, exploring, and investigating natural phenomena. The environment would be structured to deliver only the best in nutrition and health. Most importantly, when confronted with an unfamiliar question or situation, not only would they know where to look for appropriate information, they would know the appropriate questions to ask, and how to ask them.

Most children in our culture do not learn to describe physical processes adequately because they do not have a vocabulary equal to their physical abilities. They are not encouraged to formulate such descriptions in their daily lives; therefore they do not develop an appropriate, descriptive language. There is an old truism that says: Once one can correctly state the problem, a solution is not far off.

When children grow up having a physical reference for the words they use, it will provide them with a much more realistic understanding of their world and of their relationship to it. Utilizing these methods, a child will gain a propensity towards problem solving that may be utilized in varying situations in the future. Rather than reacting from an emotional or uninformed standpoint, they would tend to ask, "What is the nature of the situation?" or "What do we have here?" This unique type of education will help children become more creative and participatory members of society.

Children would learn that it takes a great many experiments and a great deal of effort to solve problems. Through this process, they realize that although they may fail initially to achieve what they set out to do, this is an acceptable part of human experience. They would be taught that in medical research and other fields it sometimes takes thousands of unsuccessful experiments before arrival at a solution. Even the experiments that fail generally succeed as essential steps in the process of achieving a goal. And sometimes other discoveries emerge along the way. The children would learn not to get discouraged with these failures, that they are an inherent part of all research and development.

Few of our schoolbooks refer to the long, tedious work required to invent an object like the light bulb. No single individual manages one, great leap in technology or science without first taking several strides. Each invention is a result of a series of progressive refinements, one upon another. Every success results from the many failures and successes that have preceded it. Unfortunately, all too often our romantic notions and egos get in the way of this understanding.

This dependency on the serial progression of creativity can easily be verified if we examine the history of invention. This same process applies to the arts and sciences.

Children will come to understand that no single entity, living or nonliving, is self-activated. This concept is referred to as the mechanistic point of view. For example, a ball does not simply roll down a hill: it is acted upon by gravity. The heat from the sun is generated by a nuclear furnace; this furnace is set in motion by immense pressure. A child will ask what makes an airplane fly, as though there were a simple answer. They ask, "Is it the propeller?" No — it requires an engine to turn a propeller. They reply, "Is it the engine?" No — the engine requires fuel. They say, "Oh, is it the fuel?" In other words, there are many interacting principals at work, involving both aerodynamics and physics. All things are acted upon by resident forces, from a single cell to the cosmos in its entirety and, as noted previously, even human behavior.

Children will learn that the assumption of a beginning or an end is a fictitious assumption. This concept is a carryover from earlier civilization's attempt to account for the nature of events in the physical world with very limited information.

Our redesigned education would be free of the influence of moribund institutions, corporate or self-interests, or any form of indoctrination of a political, national or religious nature. Similarly, the educational system would be a continuous, seamless process, the degree of each individual's curiosity enabling them to progress to the next level without grading.

Such an education would not only emphasize science and human behavior, but would also provide students with the necessary and changing professions required to maintain social and individual growth and stability in a resource-based economy. This education would enable students to engage constructively with all members of their society as well as have the ability to engage in international communication.

Some future professions would include mathematics, nanotechnology, nuclear engineering, nuclear chemistry, automation, cybernetics, systems engineering, systems analysis, remote control technology, 3-D virtual prototyping, design of plug-in components, computer-aided design and engineering, micro-machined electronic and mechanical systems, motion control, photochemical machining, ocean sciences, automated data acquisition systems, mariculture technology, simulation technology, life sciences, ecology, sociology, behavioral sciences, advanced plasma technology, industrial design, prefabrication technology, medical and bio-engineering, nutrition and health, soil enhancement systems, recycling of waste products, space science, terraforming, technology, behavioral sciences, and a host of others for which we have no name or knowledge today.

A host of other professions will disappear in a non-monetary, resource-based economy: banking, law, sales, advertising, investment brokering, real estate management, and a myriad of other occupations concerned primarily with the exclusive use of money, property and the exchange of debt.

As a student progresses from the formative stage of his/her development to the application phase, the universities and colleges of the future would not only guide students to achieve the skills relevant to an emergent society, but would also encourage them to experiment in ways that would help solve the many social problems that remain.

In the lifelong process of education, all age levels could live in cities that themselves could be designed and operated as university cities. Universities today are designed in a structured environment to provide the most advanced opportunities to facilitate education in the arts, science, music, etc. The cities in the future would be an extension of this process for fulfilling human needs. They would all serve as living universities while constantly updating information.

Much of our education today consists of a high degree of specialization, which tends to give one tunnel vision and a narrow perspective of the real interrelationships of all physical phenomena. Today it is even difficult for one schooled in sociology to communicate in depth with other members of different professions. Students of the future would be encouraged to view the world in a more holistic manner; accordingly, they would be able to converse intelligently across the various disciplines.

Children brought up in a practical, working environment of cooperation, sharing, and understanding will absorb and learn concern for their fellow human beings, reciprocating the warmth and love from all the people extensional to them. When the environment is intelligently and humanely managed, the system and the individual's behavior are mutual beneficiaries, each reinforcing and rewarding the other.

In a resource-base economy, children will live in a world with values far different then today's. As a result of this education and environment, they will possess a flexibility of attitude and mind that will enable them to evaluate new and different ideas. The earlier the exposure to science with human concern, the better prepared children will be to take a more appropriate place in the cybernated world of the near future. **Science and education, when devoid of a social conscience or environmental and human concern, are meaningless.**

CHAPTER 15

CITIES THAT THINK

ARCHITECTURE IN AN EMERGING CULTURE

We recommend that the present state and aim of architecture also be redefined to fit the needs of an emerging future. The questions we should concern ourselves with are: *What ends are these new cities to serve?* and *What are the prime considerations in designing a place of residence?*

In simplified form, a home may be any type of enclosure that protects people from varying weather conditions and provides for most of the occupant's primary needs: a place to rest, sleep, work, and carry out the business of ordinary living. We presently think of a shelter or dwelling as a suitable structure fabricated of wood, steel, concrete, and glass or a combination of materials. We envision a structure with windows to provide light and exterior walls for privacy. We install bathrooms for sanitary purposes. We utilize electricity for heating, air-conditioning and so forth. Our notions about a home generally reflect these limited concepts.

Throughout history, dwellings took many forms. People sought shelter from the effects of weather in caves. Others used a wigwam, a lean-to, and floating habitats. All manner of materials were utilized, including bamboo, clay, the sides of cliffs and hills, domes of ice, and countless others. At present people are seriously considering the possible colonization of the sea and outer space. Since shelters take so many forms, we have to broaden our expectations of shelters. Although one does not ordinarily think of an early diving suit as a shelter, it protects the wearer from the immediate surroundings, that is, from the hostile element of the sea. A space suit provides similar protection. Such suits enable people to function in an environment that does not ordinarily support life. From body enclosures to single dwellings, multiple dwellings, and eventually to total enclosure systems in which the entire city works together as a single organism — this could be the evolution of shelters.

In times to come, the effects of weather may be shielded by electronic means. The furnishings of future dwellings may consist of totally different configurations that automatically adjust to our body contours. Newer technologies may render walls entirely transparent so that occupants can view the surrounding landscape without anyone on the outside being able to see in. Daylight could be softened and subdued according to the preference of the occupants. These buildings would provide a barrier to sound, insects, and dust, and maintain the desired, optimal internal temperature. The telephone of the future might not have the physical appearance we are familiar with: it may be entirely invisible and a component part of the interior structure. It may focus sound to the proximity of your ear by electronic means. The building's materials may be energy generating and control their own, surrounding climate.

If we look upon such a dwelling with our present habits of thought, it appears unfamiliar and very different from what we are accustomed to. It may even appear, to some, to be of a surreal nature.

It is not so much that this new residence does not resemble a home, as one knows it; it is rather that it is foreign to our concept of what a home ought to be, as we understand it. We conceive our homes only within the restrictions of our own habits of thought and indoctrination.

In times to come, the definition of anything in the physical world will not be as restricted to appearance only; rather, it will be thought of in terms of the function it renders.

While some advocate the modification of existing cities and spend much time and resources attempting to update them, we find such attempts inadequate. Modification carries a large price in dollars and sustainment resources. Modifying and building on what we have means we must continue to support a combination of older systems' infrastructure and energy needs, their high cost of operation and maintenance, and their overall inefficiency, not to mention their detrimental effect on the occupants. It is actually less expensive to build newer cities from the ground up than to restore and maintain the old ones, just as it is far more efficient and less costly to design a flexible, state of the art production method than to attempt to upgrade an obsolete factory.

To live in a world without pollution and waste, yet keep parks, playgrounds, art and music centers, schools, and health care available to everyone without a price tag, profound changes are required in the way we plan our cities and conduct human affairs.

The innovative, multi-dimensional and circular cities we propose combine the most sophisticated utilization of available resources and construction techniques. The geometrically elegant, circular arrangement, surrounded by parks and gardens, is designed to operate with the minimum expenditure of energy in order to obtain the highest possible standard of living for everyone. The city would use the best of clean technology in harmony with the local ecology.

The design and development of these new cities emphasize the restoration and protection of the environment: in our view, technology without human concern is meaningless.

In a resource-based economy the circular arrangement employs a systems approach, efficiently applying resources and energy conservation, ease of fabrication and relative freedom from maintenance. The process of assembling entire cities through the standardization of basic, structural systems prefabricated in automated plants and often assembled on site, is the only feasible way to provide a very high standard of living for all people within the shortest possible time. This permits a wide range of flexibility in design and takes advantage of interchangeable units. In this way cities could take on new and different appearances depending on their function. Each would be unique. This approach does not reduce the lives of people to a subsistence level; rather, it makes available all the amenities that modern science and technology can provide. Even the wealthiest people of today could not achieve a standard of living equal to that of a resource-based economy.

Prefab modular units could converge on a building site to facilitate automatic assembly. All the electronics could be an integral part of the building of modular components, each one easily connected to existing power supplies — if the buildings are not entirely self-generating. All construction would be prescheduled to minimize interference with ongoing traffic.

The shape of tomorrow's cities — their geometry, external appearance, and the total configuration — would be a direct expression of the function they are designed to serve, keeping in mind that such a city is the extension of human activity in complete harmony with the surrounding environment. These new cities would serve as universities. Each would be designed to carry out specific, integrated functions and have a flexibility to permit changes for new and innovative installations. The size of the cities would vary depending on their geographic location and their use.

In the planning of new cities, computers would help determine the design parameters based upon the most appropriate environment to meet human and environmental needs. These total environments could be constructed to permit the widest possible range of individuality and creativity for the inhabitants.

We are often asked: Who will direct and program this cybernated city system? No-one will. The major difference between today's computer technology and the system we recommend is that our system extends its autonomic nervous system (environmental sensors) into all areas of the social complex. They function to coordinate a balance between production and distribution and operate a balanced-load economy. The decisions are arrived at on the basis of feedback from the environment.

For example, in the agricultural belt electronic probes embedded in the soil automatically maintain a constant inventory of the water table, soil conditions, nutrients, etc., and act appropriately without the need for human intervention as conditions change. This method of industrial electronic feedback could be applied to the entire system.

Another difference we propose is the reworking of concepts that drive our production planning. Instead of large, in-house facilities that create standardized products with limited application, we propose production devices that operate during the act of delivery. For example, transportation modules for ships, trains and planes that process time-sensitive products like fish and vegetables en route. The development of building materials that retain an element of fluidity would lead to the creation of indestructible houses, music centers, art centers and multi-purpose buildings in a variety of shapes and sizes.

What the new city would provide is a total environment, with clean air and water, health care, good nutrition, access to information and education for all. The city would have art and music centers, fully equipped machine shops, science labs, hobby and sports areas, and manufacturing districts. These new cities could also provide all manners of recreation within a short distance of the residential district. This type of technology is inevitable. Waste recycling, renewable and clean power generating systems, and all manner of services would be managed by integrated, cybernated methods. The management of human affairs, such as life styles and personal preferences, are totally selected by the individual.

Some of the cities could be circular, while others may be linear, underground, or constructed as floating cities in the sea. Cables and satellite positioning could be incorporated to prevent drifting for sea-borne cities.

Eventually, many cities may be designed as total enclosure systems, much like a cruise ship outfitted for a six-month cruise. They would contain residences, theaters, parks, recreation, entertainment centers, health care and educational facilities, and all the requirements for a total living environment. Everything built in these cities would be as near to a self-contained system as conditions allow. In northern locations, some could be partially underground.

The underground or subterranean city of the future could be a total-enclosure dome system. The purpose of the first, subterranean mega city might be to research the possibilities of sustaining life forms on inhospitable planets. Many underground cities could be built in inhospitable regions of our planet. They can provide an ideal climate year round with lush gardens and waterfalls. In other words, they would be able to supply all the benefits of a subtropical environment. Some of these cities would be self-sustaining and possibly generate energy from geothermal sources.

The future will generate newer materials and methods, which will result in vastly different expressions of structure, form, and function, each consistent with an evolving and changing world. Most of the new materials will probably serve multiple purposes. They could be lightweight, high strength, and low maintenance, with acoustical properties not found in today's structures. These newer materials could combine all of these factors as an integral part of the structural components.

Some new structural materials may be of a sandwich-type construction that is semi-flexible, with an inner foam core and a glazed ceramic, outer surface to allow for expansion and contraction without fracture. This will require no maintenance. Their thin shell construction can be mass-produced in a matter of hours. With this type of construction, there would be minimal damage from earthquakes, hurricanes, termites, and fires. Windows would be controlled electronically to shade or darken external illumination and come equipped with computer-controlled, automatic cleaning systems that require no human labor.

Combining innovative technologies makes it possible to conserve resources for lesser-developed regions, without sacrificing any of the conveniences of advanced living. It is only through such a process of applying innovation that our end goals of a high standard of living for the entire human race can be achieved.

We have no shortage of material. The misuse and waste of resources by our monetary-oriented society create artificial scarcity.

When we look at a city as a biome that grows and adapts, requiring energy, food and water, disposal systems, and arteries for transportation of goods and people, our ideas of space and permanency change dramatically. Our present haphazard growth patterns reflect available space and access rather than any cohesive planning. Joining the city elements together in a predetermined way conserves energy and provides easy access to all portions of the city. Most of the prefabricated elements that comprise the city would be designed to permit modification as needed. With the introduction of newer materials, the city design can be continuously updated, while taking into consideration new technological and structural progress and evolving human patterns. All systems would be of an emergent nature and constructed to allow the maximum latitude in accommodating change. This could permit the city to function as an evolving, integrated organism rather than a static structure.

Industrial construction could also be automated through the process of continuous frame structures consisting of metal, glass, plastic and reinforced, pre-stressed, lightweight concrete. These would probably be selected as universal units for constructing factories, educational facilities, harbor systems, etc. Mega-machines could construct entire buildings by computerized, pre-programmed instructions, reducing construction time considerably. This programming could be readily altered to fit changing conditions.

The architecture and individual dwellings of the future would evolve in a completely different manner from today's structures. With the intelligent application of humane technologies, we could provide a wide array of uniquely individual homes. Structural elements would be flexible and coherently arranged to best serve each individual. These prefabricated, modular homes, embodying a high degree of flexibility inconceivable in times past, could be built in any place one might imagine, whether the preference be amidst forests, atop mountains, or on remote islands.

All these dwellings can be designed as self-contained residences, with thermal generators, heat concentrators and photovoltaic arrays built into the skin of the building, and with thermo panes to tint out the bright sunlight by variable patterns of shading. All these features can be selected by the occupant, and can supply more than enough of the energy required to operate the entire household.

Buildings may also contain a precise combination of dissimilar metals utilizing the thermocouple effect for heating and cooling, and other materials embedded in solid state plastic or ceramic, structural materials. The warmer it gets on the outside, the cooler it becomes on the inside. The application of this principle can serve to heat or cool the buildings. The interiors of the homes would be designed to suit the preferences of the individuals.

TRANSPORTATION

In the new, cybernated cities of the future personal travel to distant locations may be less desirable because of the many interesting events, options, and activities immediately available near home.

When travel outside the city is desired or necessary, computer-guided vehicles for land, sea, air, space and beyond could transport passengers and freight. With the adoption of integrated transport systems passengers and freight would be moved with a minimal expenditure of energy.

For rapid movement of passengers on land across viaducts, bridges and tunnels, high-speed mag-lev trains could span great distances and replace most aircraft transportation. Some of the passenger compartments in the transport units can be lifted from the moving train in transit, eliminating waiting time at stations. Rail, sea and undersea craft could handle most freight. Many of the transport units could have detachable components and contain internationally standardized containers, each of which could be easily transferred.

In the cities, types of escalators and elevators, conveyors and transveyors, move in all directions while interconnected with all other transport systems. A circular route around the outer perimeter would connect conveyor systems to radial and vertical extensions, making it possible to travel to any part of the city quickly. Future cities can be designed to accommodate all transport systems for the convenience of passengers and freight alike.

Most of the smaller transportation units for people could be operated by voice control. When voice control is not practicable or possible, alternative methods such as keypads could be used. All transportation systems would be modular, continuously updated, and provided with the latest developments in current technology.

The transportation system within the cybernated cities of tomorrow extends to the home as well. Although all manner of goods and services would be readily available in the city center, most people, if they chose, could access materials and information from their places of residence.

CONSPICUOUS WASTE

If our civilization is to endure, it must eventually outgrow the need for conspicuous waste of time, effort, and natural resources. This may be seen in any number of areas. At one time, architectural adornments were an integral part of construction. The lofty columns and colonnaded porticos of ancient Greece and Rome were necessary components of the structures. But with the advent of newer, lightweight materials and engineering improvements, we now span greater distances without these columns or other intervening support structures. Yet the designers of many of our government buildings, including the Capitol in Washington, D.C., engage in the conscious withdrawal of efficiency to maintain designs felt to be impressive, but which actually reflect mere convention and artificiality.

Designing a building with many projections of artificiality does not indicate originality, creativity, or individuality. Individuality is expressed in our unique way of thinking about ourselves and the world around us, not in our external appearance. If we continue to design our buildings with conspicuous waste and decoration, we lessen the standard of living for others.

This is not to detract from the beautiful structures created in the past with the available and limited technology of the times. However, the continuing application of these ancient methods of construction retards the innovative and creative thinking which is necessary to an emergent culture. The intelligent use of resources incorporated into structures will considerably simplify our lifestyle and reduce waste and maintenance.

These new cities will provide for the needs of the inhabitants through the efficient allocation of resources and materials, in an energy-conscious and pollution-free environment.

In human systems, evolution distributed eyes and internal organs in a fairly uniform manor. The same is true for all plant and animal species. Uniformity is not necessarily a bad thing if it functions towards a satisfactory end. However, the dangers of uniformity are evident in our inability to shrug off useless values or methods which have outgrown their usefulness. Perhaps the only kinds of uniformity acceptable in the future will be the protection of the environment and concern for our fellow human beings.

We have to ask ourselves what kind of world we want to live in: the choice and responsibility are ours.

HOLISTIC CONSIDERATIONS IN A RESOURCE-BASED ECONOMY

In a resource-based economy, holistic considerations become an integral part of overall planning. A careful investigation of the positive and negative effects of each project would be carefully analyzed before any project is undertaken.

The cities we propose offer the possibility of tremendous intellectual growth, with its emphasis on environmental and human concern. These cities would be free of noise, pollution, most crime, and many other deleterious conditions associated with the cities of today.

Of course, people will be free to live wherever they choose. But these cities are planned with plenty of open country, parks, and wooded areas. In the areas for individual housing there will be enough vegetation and trees between houses to impart a sense of privacy.

At first glance, our proposal for a city of the future may appear impracticable; yet it represents an achievable, sustainable, and sophisticated environment, one that is designed to help bring out the best in the human potential. These cities will not only provide resources and information but will be university cities of continuous growth, designed to encourage individuality, creativity, and cooperation — with concern for the total person.

The transition to this social arrangement will not be an easy one. Never in human history has there been a smooth transition from one social system to another. Any major change engenders a certain degree of resistance. The most effective way to implement such a change is through worldwide use of media, seminars and workshops during the initial design stage

In the final analysis, talk proves little. Just as all new ideas go through a process of maturation and development, we expect our experimental City of the Future to gradually gain acceptance by fulfilling its promise as a highly successful, peaceful, and desirable place to live. As newer communities develop and become widely accepted, they will provide the basis of a new society through the process of evolution rather than revolution.

CIRCULAR CITY

The outer perimeter will be part of the recreational area with golf courses, hiking and biking trails, and opportunities for water sports. A waterway surrounds the agricultural belt with its enclosed, transparent buildings. The application of newer technologies will eliminate once and for all the use of dangerous chemicals and pesticides. Continuing into the city center, the eight green sectors provide clean renewable sources of energy with wind, thermal, and solar energy devices. The residential belt features beautiful landscaping, lakes, and winding streams. The homes and apartments will be gracefully contoured to blend in with the landscape. A wide range of innovative architecture will provide many choices for the occupants.

CIRCULAR CITY

Adjacent to the residential district, a wide selection of healthy, organically-grown food will be available on a 24-hour basis. Next are the apartments and design centers. Surrounding the central dome, eight domes house the science, art, music, research, exhibition, entertainment, and conference centers, which are all fully equipped and available to everyone.

The central dome or "theme center" houses the cybernated system, educational facilities, a health center, as well as facilities for shopping, communications, networking, and childcare. In addition, it serves as the core for most transportation services, which will take the form of horizontal, vertical, radial, and circular conveyors that safely move passengers anywhere within the city. This system facilitates efficient transportation for city residents, eliminating the need for automobiles. City-to-city transportation would be provided by monorail and electrically operated vehicles.

CYBERNATED COMPLEX

This cybernated complex utilizes advanced imaging technology to project a 3-D, "virtual" image of the earth in real time. It utilizes satellite communication systems to provide information on worldwide weather conditions, ocean currents, resource inventories, population, agricultural conditions, and fish and animal migration patterns. The interconnected, cybernated complexes represent the brain and nervous system of the entire world's civilization. All of this information will be available on demand to everyone via the Internet. This single site manages our common heritage — the resources, carrying capacity and health of the earth.

UNIVERSITY CITY

This University of Architecture and Environmental Studies, or "World University," is a testing ground for each phase of architectural development. This would be a "living," continually evolving research institute open to all. Student performance would be based on "competence accreditation" and research findings would be applied directly to the social structure to benefit all of humanity.

People will live in these experimental cities and provide feedback on the livability and serviceability of the various structures. This information would be used to formulate modifications to structures so that maximum efficiency, comfort, and safety are assured. This facility is also used to develop modular construction systems and components that serve a wide range of needs and preferences. In most instances, the external appearance of the buildings will reflect the function of the building – they are designed "from the inside out."

MILE-HIGH SKYSCRAPERS

These skyscrapers are constructed of carbon fiber-reinforced and pre-stressed concrete. They will be stabilized against earthquakes and high winds by three massive, elongated, tapered columns, which are 100 feet wide and almost a mile high. This tripod-like structure is reinforced to diminish compression, tension, and torsion stresses. These super-sized skyscrapers assure that more land will be available for parks and wilderness preserves, while concurrently helping to eliminate urban sprawl. Each one of these towers encloses a complete environment, containing a shopping center as well as childcare, educational, health, and recreational facilities. This will help alleviate the need to travel to outside facilities. Although the author is not in favor of mile-high skyscrapers, if we do not maintain a balance between the population and the earth's carrying capacity we may have to move our cities not only skyward and seaward, but subterranean as well.

CENTER FOR DIALOGUE

The directive of The Center for Dialogue would be to submit the urgent issues of the times to critical examination, and to raise relevant questions for informed public dialogue.

BUILDING OF DOMED STRUCTURES

BRIDGES

These elegant bridges are designed to carry compression, tension and torsion loads in the simplified expression of its structural members. Mag-lev trains are suspended beneath the enclosed traffic lanes.

MAG-LEV TRAINS —
MASS TRANSPORTATION SYSTEMS

While these high-speed, magnetic levitation trains are in motion, a segment of the passenger compartment can be either lifted or slid to the side. These detachable sections can then take passengers to their local destinations while other compartments are lowered in their place. This method allows the main body of the train to remain in motion saving time and enhancing efficiency. In addition, the removable compartments could be specially equipped to serve a wide range of transportation services.

AUTOMOBILES

Streamlined cars provide high-speed, energy efficient, and safe long-range transportation. Some vehicles will have wheels, while others will eventually be equipped with magnetic levitation or air-floatation capabilities. Most vehicles will be equipped with voice-recognition technology that allows the passengers to request their destination by voice command. Self-monitoring systems tell the vehicles when service is required, and they transport themselves to service and maintenance facilities. Use of clean, non-polluting electrical energy allows for silent vehicle operation, while proximity-sensor devices linked to automated velocity and braking systems enhance safety by enabling the vehicles to avoid collisions. As a secondary safety measure, the entire interior will be equipped with ergonomically-designed air bag systems. Within the cities, horizontal, vertical, radial, and circular conveyors will serve most transportation needs.

AIR TRANSPORTATION

These Vertical Takeoff and Landing (VTOL) aircraft lift passengers and freight by the use of ring-vortex air columns. The helicopter in the foreground has a stationary center around which the rotors are propelled by engines at their tips. VTOL aircraft will be propelled by a variety of techniques, from ducted fans to vectored jets. They will be designed to combine the most desirable attributes of fixed-wing aircraft, helicopters, and flying platforms. Transcontinental travel will be achieved through advanced aircraft and high-speed mag-lev trains, all integrated into a worldwide transportation system.

FUTURE AIRCRAFT

Since military aircraft will be unnecessary in the future, emphasis can be shifted to advancing medical, emergency, service, and transportation vehicles. Here is an example of VTOL (Vertical Take-off and Landing) aircraft with three synchronous turbines, which allow exceptional maneuverability. These delta-configuration aircraft can be controlled by electrodynamic means, eliminating the need for ailerons, elevators, rudders, spoilers, flaps or any other mechanical controls. In addition to providing better maneuverability and aerodynamic qualities, this innovative technology also includes a de-icing system. In the event of an emergency landing, fuel will be ejected to prevent fires.

AIRPORTS

The central dome of this airport of the future contains air terminals, maintenance facilities, service centers, and hotels. The runways are arranged in a radial configuration, which allows airplanes to easily take off into the prevailing winds and to avoid dangerous crosswind landings. Emergency stations at the edge of the runways are fully equipped with built-in fire fighting equipment and emergency arresting gear. All of the runways will be equipped with built-in sprinkler systems. Passengers will be transported to and from the airport by underground conveyors. Many of the terminals themselves will eventually be constructed underground for increased safety and better use of the land.

AUTOMATED CANALS & WATERWAYS

Included in a national transportation system would be a network of waterways, canals, and irrigation systems. We can no longer treat natural and man-made elements of the environment as stand-alone systems. These "mega hydrological projects" will be an integrated part of intercontinental planning. These bodies of water could minimize the threat of floods and droughts while allowing the migration of fish, removal of accumulated silt, and creation of sites to manage and "clean" agricultural and urban run-off. These waterways would also be part of an international flood control system that diverts floodwaters to water storage basins, allowing the water to be utilized during periods of drought. This would not only help maintain the water table,

but would also provide natural firebreaks as well as an emergency water source for fires. In addition, these canals would supply water for farming and irrigation, supply the nation's land-based fish farms, protect the wetlands and wildlife, and supply water to recreation areas.

INTERNATIONAL SHIPPING SYSTEMS

These ships will be in effect floating, automated plants, capable of processing raw materials into a finished product while en route to their destination. Some serve as industrial fish processing plants and canneries, while others would be equipped with multi-cellular compartments capable of transporting a wide variety of products.

Hydrodynamic seafaring vessels permit high-speed, efficient travel. They will be energy efficient and provide maximum comfort and safety for all passengers. They will be manufactured from durable composite materials, their outermost skin consisting of a thin layer of titanium, which requires minimal maintenance. Portions of the upper deck will slide open when the weather permits.

HOMES

The architecture and individual dwellings of future cities will evolve on an entirely different basis from today's houses. With the intelligent application of humane technologies, we will be able to provide and allow for a wide array of unique individual homes. Their structural elements will be flexible and coherently arranged to best serve individual preference. These pre-fabricated, modular homes, embodying a high degree of flexibility inconceivable in times past, could be built in any place one might imagine, amid forests, atop mountains, or on remote islands.

HOMES

Homes could be prefabricated of a new type of pre-stressed, reinforced concrete with a flexible ceramic external coating; they would be relatively maintenance-free, fireproof, and impervious to the weather. Their thin shell construction can be mass-produced in a matter of hours. With this type of construction, there would be minimal damage from earthquakes and hurricanes.

HOMES

All these dwellings can be designed as self-contained, energy efficient residences with their own thermal generators and heat concentrators. Photovoltaic arrays would be built into the skin of the building and into the widows themselves. "Thermopanes" tint out the bright sunlight by variable patterns of shading. All these features could be selected by the occupant to supply more than enough of the energy required to operate the entire household.

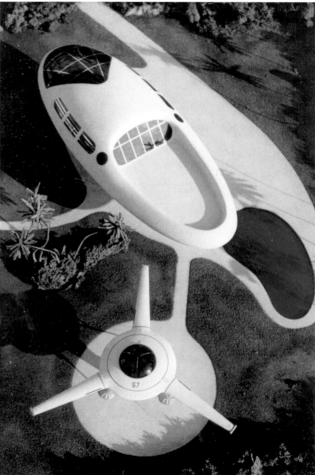

SPACE STATIONS

Space stations provide the advantages of a gravity-free research environment. They can be entirely automated and self-contained to permit maintenance and self-repair without human intervention. These space stations would be able to monitor the earth's resources, as well as facilitate further research in the fields of meteorology and astronomy, work that is often difficult on Earth due to atmospheric interference. Many other experiments can be accomplished in a gravity-free environment, particularly in the areas of medicine, chemistry, and metallurgy. In addition, these space stations would serve as nodes in a worldwide telecommunications system, providing up-to-date information on the Earth's ecosystems, the position of ships and airliners, and other information pertinent to the inhabitants of the cybernated world.

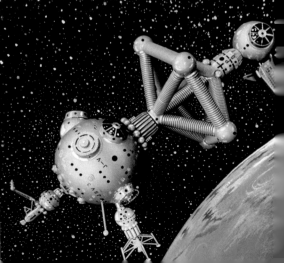

CHAPTER 16

LIFESTYLE IN THE FUTURE

FAMILY MATTERS

THE MEDIA AND POLITICIANS TALK A LOT about the dissolution of conventional family structure, and the societal values associated with it. They see the family as the primary, most basic venue for acquiring such life skills as sociability, responsibility, stability, and concern for others. The increasing unrest and lack of direction exhibited by many young people seem to validate these concerns for them.

At present, it is necessary for both husbands and wives to work. Monetary economics have to a large extent undermined family cohesion and childcare. Parents lack adequate time to spend with their children, and they are constantly stressed by ever-rising medical bills, insurance payments, educational expenses, and cost of living expenses. Ironically, for many, one of their most pressing expenses is childcare, to pay for which they must go to work.

It is in this area that one of the most profound benefits of this new civilization could be realized. Shorter workdays will provide greater opportunities for family members to peruse their areas of personal interest. Free access to goods and services will make the home a much more pleasant place, with the removal of the economic stress that causes so much family turmoil.

The question arises: Would people be happier in this kind of society? Perhaps it isn't so much happiness that we seek: happiness is relative to each individual's distinct nature, and is thus individually defined and achieved. We seek to create a society where people are free to choose their own areas of interest, develop formerly hidden potential, and pursue their dreams without government intervention or financial constraint.

CHANGING VALUES IN A CYBERNATED SOCIETY

As of this writing, the vision of the good life in industrial nations, particularly the United States, entails productive and rewarding employment, a healthy existence, perhaps a home in the suburbs and a second in the country, money in the bank, good education, pleasant family relations, healthy and intelligent children, and the guarantee of a secure future. This projected fantasy is an elusive goal for almost all people.

Tomorrow's vision of the good life may differ considerably. With the elimination of scarcity, and when most material needs are met by a world resource-based economy, we may reasonably expect to see considerable improvement in living conditions and opportunities for a meaningful and productive life for all people.

Consider for the moment what the world could be like if most physical needs are met. What will happen to individuality and human values in a world of unlimited abundance?

Rather than evolving into an age of dynamic leisure, truly intelligent and committed people find very little free time, even if they don't have to "work" for a living. The energies, once devoted to dealing with the myriad problems of material scarcity, could now be directed toward self-development and fulfillment. People would then have the means and the time for intellectual and spiritual growth, and the time to realize what it really means to be human in a caring society. When social affairs are consistent with the carrying capacity of the earth's resources, human beings will evolve a sense of relevance and understanding far beyond that which is possible today.

All people are culture-bound. We are victims of indoctrination and of our social customs. Most of us would be bewildered and even uncomfortable with the flexibility of a new orientation. Today most of us live in economic and mental straitjackets that limit our ability to work through our problems. For the first time in human history the cybernated world offers us the opportunity to choose whatever constructive lifestyles we wish. All individual lifestyles would be determined by one's varied and changing preferences, and not by what someone else thinks is good for one.

An example of the wide range of choices that may be available in a resource-based economy would be in the way one selects a house. For instance, a man and woman may visit an architectural design center where they sit in front of a clear hemisphere approximately six feet in diameter. The woman describes the type of house she would prefer to live in and her areas of interest. The house appears as a 3-dimensional image in the center of the hemisphere. It rotates slowly to present an overview of the interior and exterior. Then the man describes his major areas of interests and preferences and suggests a larger balcony. The 3-dimensional image is adjusted. When they have finished requesting changes, the computer presents various alternatives to consider. Also, if they wish, they can enter a sensorium to experience a walk-through of their preferred design and continue to make changes.

When they arrive at the desired design, then the construction procedures are set in motion. The computer selects materials for efficiency and durability. None of the architecture is permanent and can be modified and updated at the request of the occupants.

This is real, individual choice. In a monetary system, most of us live near our work with a house, car and lifestyle we can afford (or, all too often, cannot afford), rather than the one we prefer. The truth is, we are essentially only as free as our purchasing power permits. Even many wealthy people today select a residence solely to impress others with their status. Not having a true sense of self worth, many live to impress others.

A resource-based economy changes the function of our dwellings from that of status symbol or basic shelter to a reflection of our individuality and interests.

A resource-based economy would provide art centers, music centers, theater projects, and an opportunity for all people to return to an educational environment, travel, and pursue their interests. Although people would be economically secure, they would still need real challenges to maintain incentives and enhance creativity. The future will offer these challenges in abundance.

CHAPTER 17

FUTURE POSSIBILITIES

NO ONE CAN ACTUALLY FORETELL THE FUTURE in education, science, and technology with precision. There are too many variables involved, and with the advent of newer developments there follows an exponential rise in the learning curve. Therefore we can only extrapolate change based on current trends. Although this method has its limitations, it is the best that we have at present. The future will generate its own values.

The following projections of the future have little to do with the current scenarios popularized in mainstream publications: gadgets and gimmicks available only to upscale, high-income households such as high-tech kitchens with appliances that "talk" and "think"; more advanced and sophisticated weapons, warplanes and ships; and enhanced personal security systems. All these are relevant to a scarcity-oriented culture, and the need, even the desire for many of them disappears with the implementation of a resource-based economy.

One of the major developments of the future will be the field of Informatics, the science of relevant information. We are already moving from data access to management of information. The Internet and information technology allow us to create and use "stateless" information — new information we create by combining data and information from separate data systems and web sites. Development is also ongoing in knowledge management, although most efforts focus on archiving documents and processes. In a monetary-based society, this is logical. These are "seeable" products. True knowledge management allows unconstrained and simplified access to vast amounts of pertinent information.

In addition, nanotechnology shows enormous potential. Nanotechnology combines optics with lasers. This technology will enable us to assemble matter, atom by atom, into whatever molecular configuration is needed. Even today a variety of micro machines, some far smaller than a grain of sand, are part of our technology. This technology is capable of propelling a tiny turbine made of a silicone compound. When a laser illuminates the turbine and the beam is focused at the turbine blades, these micro machines spin rapidly and can be used for many different purposes.

Other micro machines would be used to clear plaque from blood vessels and perform pre-programmed surgical procedures. Eventually medical nano-replicators may replace damaged or non-functioning organs. Some may even outperform the replaced organ. This includes livers, hearts, eyes, brain tissue, and more. Nanotechnology will lead to a sub-microscopic revolution, not only in the field of medicine but in industry as well.

In the industrial sector production machines would become much more versatile; dies would be programmed to assume any required configuration by varying the molecular bond, while maintaining the accuracy of the system throughout the production process. Each machine becomes faster and more versatile, performing an almost unlimited range of tasks. Noise abatement systems will be used throughout the industrial environment.

Eventually, the need for the transportation of goods and services would also diminish. Products could be replicated and produced within one's own community, eventually within one's own home.

With other forms of energy we would be able to explore outer space. Intelligent robots and mega machines would "terraform" (that is, modify) the uninhabitable planets above ground and underground to support human and plant life and provide all the necessary conditions to sustain human colonization.

The replacement of paperwork by computerized technologies enabled industries to save thousands of feet of the space formerly used to house documents. This also eliminated thousands of clerks and secretaries. Microchip technology freed more than seventy percent of the storage space formerly needed. At present, millions of people throughout the world access electronic information storage systems from their homes or from anywhere else they may be. These information storage systems will continue to shrink, especially with the advances in nanotechnology. What may occupy thousands of square feet of storage space today with molecular information storage systems will be able to fit on the head of pin.

People could have microscopic implants so that, in the event of an accident, when they arrive at a hospital the implant could instantly download all the relevant medical information about the individual. This would eliminate all emergency room paperwork and make the diagnoses much faster and easier to perform.

Another fascinating process is advanced shape memory in plastics, metals and other materials. This process will probably lead to sub-microscopic, electro-morphic materials. Such materials will be able to alter their external appearance to whatever shape will produce the best performance. Most home furnishings in the future would be capable of adjusting their shapes to accommodate the human body.

Other aspects of the future would be realistic, 3-D visualization with teletactile and olfactory enhancements that could enable one to touch and smell flowers or any other visual representations, from the undersea world to the stars.

With the advent of artificial intelligence, the technological performance of machines will outpace/outperform the need for managerial oversight. Molecular circuitry will eventually provide the necessary interface to enable human beings to engage in an intelligent discourse with a machine. This technology would enable the machine to repeat and understand any written or spoken language in the world — including sign language or Braille — and permit instantaneous translation throughout the world. These same implants could be capable of doing research in all branches of the physical sciences.

Not only will this newer technology replace humans in the production sequences, but in the service sectors as well.

The introduction of this and other computer-generated technologies for multi-media application could affect the future of entertainment, resulting in 3-D, teletactile and olfactory images that simulate living beings and locations. The results could be so life-like, it would be almost impossible to separate simulation from reality.

With teletactile simulation in the projection of a human image, we will actually be able to shake hands with our virtual visitors and even walk with them through our gardens. These virtual visitors would be able to "pick up" objects and examine them. They would appear not as synthetic projections but as living, breathing, human beings.

Today we can only imagine what teletactile imaging could mean to people who have lost loved ones or who have lost limbs or their eyesight. It also opens the possibility of being in many different places at the same time, a scenario once considered an absolute impossibility. This occurs on a very primitive level today through the electronic media, when the president addresses the nations of the world.

If this boggles the minds of forward-thinking people, think what it could do to our culture-bound, rigid notions of reality. Regardless of our personal views regarding the worth or the value of this technology, it is coming. We already live in a world where yesterday's fantasies have been surpassed by today's realities.

Probably the only thing we can know for sure about the future is that it will be very different from the world today. But whatever difficulties we have trying to understand life in the future, it is nothing compared to the difficulty people of the future will have understanding the way we do things today. They will most likely find it hard to believe that human beings could have organized themselves in such an absurd fashion into nations, after which they set about using scientifically-designed weapons to slaughter each other. As they watch movies of the past they will probably be astounded at the tobacco smoke emanating from people's nostrils and the ostentatious clothing and omnipresent jewelry. They will find our simple, animal-like emotions of hostility, rage, and jealousy incredible. People in the future will probably not look back with nostalgia to a world threatened by atomic oblivion, environmental degradation, and economic and political activities permeated by greed and self-centeredness. How simple, how crude and pathetic we will appear in the eyes of our descendants — perhaps just as strange and unpleasant a sight as that of our own imaginings about *our* primitive ancestors.

When biological technology becomes further advanced, human beings as we know them will become a modified species. If we as human beings fail to include the possibility of this development in our overall, social evolution we will witness the decline of our species. All aspects of social innovation must be able to allow for change in a constantly evolving world.

CHAPTER 18

THE OCEAN FRONTIERS
OF TOMORROW

THE WEB OF LIFE ON OUR PLANET is supported by the hydro-cycle, that great
variation of forms of water which are part of the planetary circulation: the oceans, snow,
ice, rain, lakes, groundwater, and aquifers. This constantly renewed circulation, powered by
the heat of the sun, the rotation of the earth, and Coriolis forces, supports the entire life
cycle, including humankind.

We often speak of underdeveloped land areas, but rarely of the greatest undeveloped
natural resource on the planet — the world's oceans. Although humans have used the oceans
of the world for thousands of years as a source of food and transportation, we are only now
beginning to recognize the enormous potential and diversity of this relatively untapped
resource. The oceans offer an almost limitless environment for food, energy production,
minerals, pharmaceuticals, and much more.

The ocean is the only resource that has kept ahead of the population explosion. And
yet we see little regard for ocean life, which is essential to all life on Earth. In August 1970,
the U.S. Army deliberately dumped containers holding 67 tons of nerve gas into the
Atlantic Ocean. Add to this the fact that the dumping ground was close to a main artery
in this life support system, the Gulf Stream. The navies of the world, the fishing fleets,
cruise lines and many coastal cities casually use the ocean as both trashcan and toilet.

If intelligently-managed, the oceans could easily supply more than enough resources
to feed the world's hungry. Billions depend on the sea for their primary source of protein.
Life is abundant and varied here. But mismanagement of run-off created huge, lifeless areas
in the Gulf of Mexico where the Mississippi River drains. Major marine species and the
coral reefs that nurture them are rapidly disappearing — not naturally or because their
death in any way prolongs our way of life. On the contrary, these extinctions endanger us
and derive from our own arrogance and ignorance. Even amid the most complex, living
ecology, we act as predators rather than the symbiots we are.

Although the overwhelming majority of sea life dwells near the surface, in the chill,
murky depths miles below, where even sunlight never ventures, life abounds despite fantastic pressures and temperatures. In near-freezing temperatures, boiling vents of toxic gasses
support a wide array of sea life we have only begun to study.

Great rivers cross the oceans of our planet, set in motion by the earth's rotation. These immense, oceanic currents travel at varying speeds, at different depths, and even in opposite directions. It has been estimated that the Gulf Stream carries about 30 million cubic meters of water per second past Miami, Florida. This is more than five times the combined flow of all the fresh water rivers of the world. If this potential energy were harnessed, it is estimated that the project would deliver close to a thousand million watts on a 24-hour basis or as much as 2 large nuclear plants, without environmental contamination or radiation danger.

In addition powerful winds, waves, and currents provide enormous potential for the generation of electric power. The vast potential of the seas can also be realized by the production of energy crops from biomass by converting waste organic materials into gaseous or liquid fuels.

On the sea floors, and in the brine-filled waters themselves, we find a vast storehouse of metals and minerals that may be used to help resolve resource shortages. However, "harvesting" the metals and minerals will require new technologies that do not disturb the fragile sea floor.

CITIES IN THE SEA

Colonization of the oceans is one of the last frontiers that remain on earth. In the redesign of our cities, prodigious oceanic city-communities may evolve. To fully utilize this bountiful wellspring of resource, the way of the future embraces the development of large marine structures designed to explore the relatively untapped riches of the world's oceans. These cities in the sea could provide improved mariculture, fresh water production, power, and a variety of mining, which could offset land-based mining shortages. They could provide almost unlimited riches in pharmaceuticals, chemicals, fertilizers, minerals, oil, natural gas, sweet water, and tidal and wind power, to name only a few. Ocean-based and space-borne sensors will constantly track tidal flow, marine life, water composition and temperature, atmospheric conditions, and a myriad other vital signs.

Ultimately the development of these ocean communities will greatly relieve the land-based population pressures. The population of such cities would vary from several hundred to many thousand and would be located throughout the world. These will all be controlled, managed and operated by automated systems and be part of the international communications networking.

USE

Some of these cities can serve as universities and research centers where students from all nations of the world study marine sciences and management. They could also serve as monitoring stations of ocean currents, weather patterns, marine ecology, pollution, and geologic phenomena. For additional marine exploration, robotic submersibles would be available. The oceans are, after all, essential to our survival and a critical part of the earth's carrying capacity.

Other sea platforms can be used as rocket-launching systems. Space vehicles launched at the equator save a great deal of energy because the equator is the fastest moving portion of the earth. Locating launch sites there takes full advantage of the earth's rotation for additional thrust. This requires fewer thruster burns to reach geocentric orbit, or the orbit whereby a satellite rotates with the earth and remains in a stationary position relative to it.

For polar orbits, the launch platforms could be located off the West Coast of the U.S. The computerized control and command systems could be located on ships or on the platforms themselves.

Still other areas of the oceans would remain largely untouched. These are treasures in themselves and need never be turned over to technological development or exploitation. Their reclamation, enhancement, and preservation should be a priority for global conservation.

The Caribbean and the emerald shoals of the vast banks of Eleuthera feature some of the clearest waters in the Bahamas and one of the most beautiful coral atolls in the Western Hemisphere. The waters surrounding these islands vary in hue from the magnificent deep blue of the Gulf Stream to shimmering shades of green. Similar areas exist in the South Pacific and many other locations throughout the world, where thousands of miles of shoreline remain unmarred by signs of human habitation. In the new spirit of world cooperation, some of these areas could be set aside as international marine parks for the education and enjoyment of all, inviolate from exploitation. In these areas, the only human intervention taken would be measures to preserve and protect these aquatic sanctuaries.

LIFESTYLES ON THE SEA CITIES

Cities of the sea could offer new and fascinating lifestyles for millions of inhabitants, while easing the land-based population pressure. Massive ocean structures would be both above and beneath the sea. These structures would represent a spectacular engineering achievement with aircraft, sea craft and submersible access.

Some of these cities in the sea could also serve as underwater international parks where visitors could observe the great protected reefs of the world. Through huge undersea windows they would be able to view the wonders of this environment in leisure and comfort; from a computerized chair, they could communicate with dolphins and other forms of marine life, while the more daring among them could leave the premises by way of airlocks and go on diving expeditions.

CONSTRUCTION

Cities in the sea could be among the greatest achievements of the twenty-first century. One of the most efficient designs would be a circular configuration, multi-storied and fabricated of steel, with glass of superior strength and pre-stressed concrete reinforced with carbon fibers.

Some may be floating versions while others could be built on pilings, with flotation barriers that would prevent wind and heavy seas from damaging the structures. In deeper waters, the floating platforms could be anchored to the seabed. Other ocean platforms could float freely. These platforms would be self-propelled and extremely stable, ballasted by columns about 20' feet in diameter that penetrate 150' below the surface. In the lower portions of these floating, cylindrical columns are a series of disks that extend out about 6 feet, spaced approximately 10' apart. These disks tend to keep the platform steady in any type of adverse weather conditions. A belt surrounding the entire project or other devices act as a breakwater.

Some of these cities can be constructed in technically developed countries and towed to their destination in sections or as complete operating systems, similar to the manner in which oil platforms are transported to their destinations today. Other configurations can be designed as variable composite structures, assembled on site and modified to serve many different functions. They can also be disassembled and relocated if required. They would vary in size depending on their function and could be as large as three-quarters of a mile in diameter with flexible interconnections.

Other above-surface structures anchored to the seabed could serve as efficient bases for mining operations. These dome-shaped structures would be totally automated, their flotation levels adjusted by flooding or emptying their buoyancy chambers. They may be constructed on land and towed to their destination, where they can be submerged and anchored in place. From the tops of these structures, a cylindrical concrete conduit will extend 150 feet above the ocean surface, its surface-base encircled by a floating dock system which would rise and fall with the tides and accommodate both surface and submersible craft.

All marine development must be in full accord with the total carrying capacity and sustainment of the ocean environment. *Before initiating any of these major projects, it is imperative to take into account the possible negative impact on the entire hydrosphere — the rivers, estuaries, lakes and oceans*

ENERGY

On these and other floating cities or platforms powerful wind turbines could capture the ocean breezes. Solar and wind power generators would be located on most of the upper decks. Cold water from the depths of the ocean can also be pumped up for various uses such as the conversion of this heat differential into electrical energy. This process could provide a continuous supply of electricity far in excess of the cities' needs.

With our dwindling agricultural space, ocean farming offers an area for unlimited energy crops. Biomass and processing of waste organic materials into liquid or gaseous fuel would provide additional energy from the fermentation processes.

MARICULTURE

Mariculture, the planned cultivation of marine crops, and fish farming communities can be designed to support more than one type of marine life. Many of these communities could maintain a balance of species in a mutually supporting, symbiotic relationship, while emulating natural conditions as closely as possible.

A wide variety of aquatic plants could also be cultivated in multiple layers, and suspended by cables in underwater fields adjacent to these cities. In some instances the tops of the plants could be harvested automatically, leaving the roots and the lower third of the plant to grow new crops without replanting.

These floating ocean platforms could also be equipped with solar-operated desalinization plants, which extract fresh water for hydroponics farming and other uses. Upwelling can also be harnessed to extract deep-sea nutrients to supply aquaculture farming. Of course, any attempt at aquaculture or mariculture must be subject to the international monitoring of ocean farms.

This would not only provide fish farming complexes, but could introduce the most advanced principles of poly-culture to maintain the reproduction and natural balance of species. Every precaution must be taken to avoid disrupting or spoiling the very spawning grounds that have sustained the human race for countless centuries.

TRANSPORTATION

Immense, floating structures would be equipped with loading and docking facilities for vessels. Huge ships that serve as processing plants could transport passengers and freight to these cities in the sea.

The upper deck would be equipped with a landing area for helicopters or VTOL aircraft. Computerized lift-units could facilitate vertical, horizontal and radial travel within these structures.

JOINT VENTURE

Ocean cities will help to provide additional food and resources for the needs of the world. Cities in space, on land, and in the oceans can be managed by a global resource management system, thus serving every nation of the world while maximizing the well-being of everyone.

Where a project of this magnitude is concerned, it is imperative that its benefits be shared equally by the entire global community. Eventually, mineral wealth of the oceans and the other resources of our world must be shared by all nations as the common heritage of humankind. If we fail to adopt these measures, the rapid exploitation and deterioration of the ocean's resources may not be reversible.

OFF SHORE APARTMENTS

Offshore apartment buildings of concrete, steel, glass, titanium, and a wide variety of new synthetic materials can be built to relieve the population pressure in areas like Hong Kong, Tokyo, Los Angeles, and New York. The materials used in such projects would be engineered to withstand the corrosive effects of the harsh ocean environment.

ARTIFICIAL ISLANDS IN THE SEA

This artificial island in the sea is designed to serve the oceanographic sciences. Multiple docking and landing facilities for VTOL aircraft surround the entire island. Water-based recreation will be a part of life in these water-borne communities. People will be able to participate in research, sailing, scuba diving, and many other surface and sub-surface activities without disturbing the balance of the marine environment.

MARICULTURE & SEA FARMING

This is a conceptual view of a mariculture and sea-farming system. Such systems cultivate and raise fish and other forms of marine life to help meet the nutritional needs of the world's people. Capable of cultivating a great variety of marine life, these structures would be equipped to permit the free flow of water throughout. They are designed to be a non-contaminating, integral part of the marine environment.

OCEAN MINING MEGA-STRUCTURES

These "cities in the sea" provide improved mariculture, fresh water production, power, and deep-ocean mining, which can help alleviate shortages of land-based minerals. Such structures could provide us with almost unlimited resources: pharmaceuticals, chemicals, fertilizers, minerals, metals, oil, natural gas, drinking water, ocean farming, as well as tidal and wind power and more.

SOCIOCYBERNEERING

SCALE: 1/2"=1'-0"

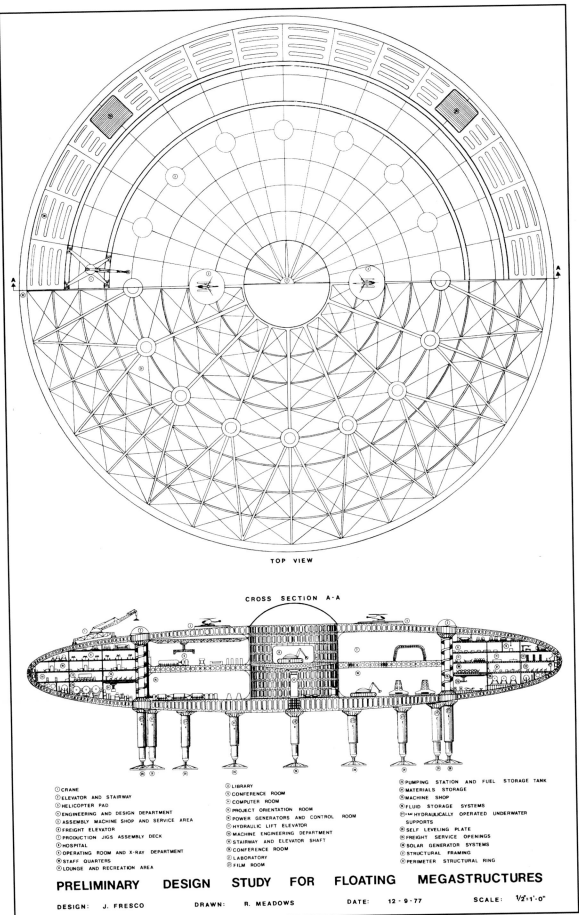

TOP VIEW

CROSS SECTION A-A

① CRANE
② ELEVATOR AND STAIRWAY
③ HELICOPTER PAD
④ ENGINEERING AND DESIGN DEPARTMENT
⑤ ASSEMBLY MACHINE SHOP AND SERVICE AREA
⑥ FREIGHT ELEVATOR
⑦ PRODUCTION JIGS ASSEMBLY DECK
⑧ HOSPITAL
⑨ OPERATING ROOM AND X-RAY DEPARTMENT
⑩ STAFF QUARTERS
⑪ LOUNGE AND RECREATION AREA

⑫ LIBRARY
⑬ CONFERENCE ROOM
⑭ COMPUTER ROOM
⑮ PROJECT ORIENTATION ROOM
⑯ POWER GENERATORS AND CONTROL ROOM
⑰ HYDRAULIC LIFT ELEVATOR
⑱ MACHINE ENGINEERING DEPARTMENT
⑲ STAIRWAY AND ELEVATOR SHAFT
⑳ CONFERENCE ROOM
㉑ LABORATORY
㉒ FILM ROOM

㉓ PUMPING STATION AND FUEL STORAGE TANK
㉔ MATERIALS STORAGE
㉕ MACHINE SHOP
㉖ FLUID STORAGE SYSTEMS
㉗ HYDRAULICALLY OPERATED UNDERWATER SUPPORTS
㉘ SELF LEVELING PLATE
㉙ FREIGHT SERVICE OPENINGS
㉚ SOLAR GENERATOR SYSTEMS
㉛ STRUCTURAL FRAMING
㉜ PERIMETER STRUCTURAL RING

PRELIMINARY DESIGN STUDY FOR FLOATING MEGASTRUCTURES

DESIGN: J. FRESCO   DRAWN: R. MEADOWS   DATE: 12-9-77   SCALE: 1/2"=1'-0"

CITIES IN THE SEA

Thousands of self-sufficient cities in the sea, varying in design according to their location and function, will eventually alleviate land-based population pressures. Some will serve as oceanographic universities to survey and maintain a dynamic balance in the oceanographic environment.

CONSTRUCTION OF A FLOATING MEGA-STRUCTURE

This illustration depicts a "floating mega-structure" that is being assembled in a dry dock entirely by robotized, automated systems free of any human intervention. After construction, these structures could be towed in sections or as completed units to locations where they would be anchored to the seabed. In some instances these cities could even travel and relocate.

CITY IN THE SEA WITH A MODULAR FREIGHTER

This modular freighter, leaving a city in the sea, consists of detachable sections that can be rapidly loaded or unloaded. The number of sections varies, depending on the amount of freight to be delivered. When all the modules are connected they can be propelled as a single unit. When the freight arrives at its destination, the selected modules can be disconnected and towed to docks.

FLOATING SEA DOMES

These unsinkable, floating sea domes will house those who prefer unique offshore or island living. In the event of severely inclement weather, they could easily be towed ashore, mounted and locked to elevated support structures. They are all equipped with retractable enclosures that cover the outer deck.

UNDERSEA OBSERVATORIES

Elevators transport visitors to underwater oceanographic viewing or research facilities. An extended under-water tunnel connects to other aquatic facilities and provides expansive, panoramic viewing of the undersea world in its natural habitat without disturbing the ocean environment.

CHAPTER 19

BEYOND UTOPIA

IN 1898, EDWARD BELLAMY wrote the book *Looking Backwards*. It presented a social system with many advanced ideas for its time. This best seller generated a great deal of interest and many people wrote to ask how the type of cooperative society Bellamy envisioned could be brought about. But our nation at that time was not prepared for a transition of this magnitude.

The proposals he presented, and those of Plato's *Republic*, the writings of Karl Marx, H. G. Wells in his book *The Shape of Things to Come*, and many others all represent attempts to find workable solutions to the many problems that earlier civilizations have left unresolved. There is little doubt that at the time of Bellamy's books, social conditions were abominable, which made the Utopian ideal much more appealing. What appears to be lacking in most of these concepts, however, is any type of plan or process to facilitate the transition. Most of the early visions of Utopia did not allow for changes in either technology or human values, tending to arrest any innovative efforts. And all have lacked a set of blueprints and methodology for implementing the ideas in a comprehensive form, and a competent staff to effect the transition.

Now, at last, we have such a vision and the means to make it a reality. In recent times we have evolved the necessary technology to surpass the fondest hopes and dreams of any social innovators of the past. Although many of the concepts presented in this book may appear to people of the early twenty-first century to be unattainable goals, all of these concepts are based upon known scientific principles. The only limitations upon the future of humankind are those that we impose upon ourselves.

The social direction we speak of has no parallel in history with any other previous political ideology or economic strategy. Just because previous attempts failed, however, is not an acceptable reason to stop trying. The real danger lies in doing nothing.

Determining the parameters of this new civilization will require a break with many of the traditions of the past. The future will evolve its own new paradigms that will hopefully fit each, successive phase of human development.

Perhaps a major influence on the origins of the earliest Utopian concepts were some of the world's religious teachings. In these imagined visions of heaven there were no property lines, banks, money, police, prisons, militarism, or private ownership.

Not so many years ago an attempt was made in the U.S. to understand a social system very different from our own. A film called *"The March of Time"* had this to say about Soviet Communism: "We believe that the American free-enterprise system will function better than the collective system. However, we wish you the best of luck on your new and unusual social experiment." The failure of communism to provide for human needs and to enrich the lives of its citizens is not unlike our own failures. In all established social systems it is necessary to devise different approaches to improve the workings of the system.

Thousands of failures occurred before the first workable airplane was produced. Dr. Erlich attempted over 606 different approaches to controlling syphilis before one finally proved successful. Some of the technology we use today, such as televisions, radios, aircraft, and automobiles are in a constant state of improvement and modification. Yet our social system remains largely static.

An inscription on one of our government buildings reads as follows: "Where there is no vision the people perish." The major reason for resisting change is that it tends to threaten the vested interests. The fear of social change is unfounded, because the history of civilization is one continuous experiment. Even the American free-enterprise system, during its earliest stages, faced a multitude of problems even more severe than they are today — long hours, exploitation of child labor, inadequate ventilation in industrial plants, lack of rights for women and black Americans, hazardous conditions in mines, and racial prejudice. Despite its many problems, it was the greatest attempt in history in terms of innovation in lifestyle, architecture, technology, and the general pursuit of progress. All we recommend is that we continue our process of social experimentation to transcend the limitations of our current society and enhance the lives of everyone.

Our future does not depend on present-day beliefs or social customs, but will continue to evolve a set of values unique to its own time. There are no Utopias. The very notion of "Utopia" is static. However, the survival of any social system ultimately depends upon its ability to allow for change to improve society as a whole.

CHAPTER 20

THE VENUS PROJECT DIRECTION

THE VENUS PROJECT IS AN ORGANIZATION based on the ideas, designs and direction presented in this book, representing the life's work of its originator and Project Director, Jacque Fresco. Its 25-acre research and design center is located in Venus, Florida, where the future is taking shape now. *The Venus Project's* purpose is to design, develop, and prepare plans to build the first experimental city. Here we are developing alternative energy systems, city designs, transportation, manufacturing methods, and more. Along with this research we are creating blueprints, renderings and models, while holding seminars and producing books, videos and other written material to introduce people to the aims of *The Venus Project* and our vision for the future.

Without reservation, we conclude that *The Venus Project* cannot be accomplished within a monetary-based society. It would take too many years for any significant changes. Any attempt to adapt our goals to a monetary-based system would water them down to such an extent that the changes would be insignificant.

As emphasized earlier in the book, it is no longer the repetitious work of just the laborers that automation will continue to phase out, but also that of engineers, technicians, scientists, doctors, architects, artists and actors as well. All of these professions will be a short-lived means of providing purchasing power. It is simply a matter of time before automated systems provide nearly all necessary services and products. Virtually all tasks presently performed by human intelligence could be performed by automated systems. This need not be a cause for alarm. In a cybernated, resource-based culture, human work will be involved in creative endeavor and problem solving. There appears to be no limit to the services and benefits for all human beings that can be performed by computerized technologies and *AI*.

The Venus Project calls for a straightforward approach to the redesign of a culture, in which the age-old inadequacies of war, poverty, hunger, debt, environmental degradation and unnecessary human suffering are viewed not only as avoidable, but totally unacceptable.

If we are sincere and genuinely concerned with resolving most of our problems, we must strive towards having the Earth's resources declared as the common heritage of all the world's people. For the reasons discussed in this book, anything less will simply result in a continuation of the problems inherent in our present system.

To effect a transition from our present, politically incompetent, scarcity-oriented and near-obsolete culture to a more humane society will require a quantum leap in both thought and action. Until recently, change came slowly. One group of incompetent leaders merely replaces another. The problems we face today cannot be solved politically or financially. Our problems are highly technical in nature and require fundamental changes in our thinking and values. There is not even enough money available to pay for the required changes, but there are **more than enough resources**. This is why *The Venus Project* advocates the transition from a monetary-based society to the eventual realization of a resource-based world economy.

The money-based system evolved centuries ago. All the worlds economic systems — socialism, communism, fascism, and even our free enterprise system — perpetuate social stratification, elitism, nationalism, oppression and racism, based primarily on economic disparity. Power relates to an individual's or group's ability to withhold food, shelter, health care, education and resources from the poor and disadvantaged. The basic sustaining factors of life are held hostage for hours of labor, as represented by a salary. Consequently, as long as a social system uses money or barter people and nations will seek to maintain the economic competitive edge; if they cannot do so by means of commerce they will attempt to do so by means of boycotts, blockades, or military intervention. Even at the time of this writing, three major economic boycotts and multiple military interventions are in progress around the world.

All social systems, regardless of political philosophy, religious beliefs, or social customs, ultimately depend upon natural resources, clean air and water, arable land, and the necessary technology and personnel to maintain and secure a high standard of living.

The Venus Project concludes that the Earth is abundant with plentiful resources. Our practice of rationing resources through monetary control is irrelevant and counter-productive to our survival.

Modern society has access to highly-advanced technologies that can provide sufficient food, clothing, housing, medical care, education, and the development of a limitless supply of renewable, non-contaminating energy sources. We have the technology, resources and personnel for everyone to enjoy a very high standard of living with all of the amenities a prosperous, global civilization can provide. *This can be accomplished through the humane and intelligent application of science and technology, based upon the existing carrying capacity of the Earth.*

The Venus Project posits that the necessary technology already exists to begin making maximum resources available and to provide food, clean air and water, comfortable housing and transportation, quality health care, environmental stability, and unlimited opportunities for personal growth to all people, not just a selected few.

Our understanding of the applications of technology suggests the possibility of eliminating scarcity by applying renewable sources of energy; humane and intelligent resource management along with the infusion of cybernation will help maintain a balanced-load economy and a far more equitable distribution of the world's resources.

Machines will monitor production and delivery of goods and services, and maintain the protection of the global environment. They will not monitor people. In a resource-based economy, monitoring people is not only socially offensive but also counterproductive.

In a saner and more humane civilization, competent use of machines would shorten the workday, increase the availability of goods and services, and lengthen vacation time. If we utilize new technology to raise the standard of living for all people, the infusion of machine technology would no longer be perceived as a threat. We would work towards replacing most forms of human labor, in its place providing challenging, interesting pursuits in problem solving and creative effort, while encouraging individuality and new incentives. The purpose of all this organized technology is to free people from the monotonous and boring work-a-day world and to enable them to pursue a more meaningful life.

Today, financial barriers place enormous limitations on innovation, development, individual creativity, and incentive. In the world envisioned by *The Venus Project*, people are free of the constraints of profit and control, and are able to explore new dimensions in human existence and pursue knowledge in the arts, sciences, or any other areas of their choice. There is a tremendous, undeveloped potential in all human beings, which is not nurtured in a monetary-based society. All would benefit by the fruition of new ideas. In a resource-based society, the measure of success would be the fulfillment of one's individual preferences and pursuits rather than the acquisition of wealth, property, and power.

HOW WE GET FROM HERE TO THERE

The Venus Project is in the process of introducing a set of values and procedures that may enable us to achieve social nucleation. Our project will provide the designs and blueprints for a prototype community to test the validity of our proposals; we will strive to achieve a relevant orientation by which people may adapt intellectually and emotionally to our new technological age. We feel that anything short of overall social design would be inappropriate and ineffective.

Since we begin in a monetary-based society, the means for raising funds to construct this experimental community can be accomplished in several different ways.

One is through the production of a major motion picture depicting the advantages of this new social system for all the world's people. Another possibility is the building of a theme park where visitors would actually experience some of the many benefits of *The Venus Project's* proposals. Books, videos, blueprints, models, a movie script, and the 25-acre research and development center have already been completed.

Any funds raised by these proposed projects, along with contributions, publications, videos, seminars, lectures, and grants, will be used to help initiate and construct the first experimental city.

Our proposals are submitted to the general public and to all educational institutions. We invite your participation. If enough people find the proposals acceptable and join with us in this new advocacy, we could form the nucleus of an organization to more forcefully implement the aims of *The Venus Project.*

EXPERIMENTAL CITY

The Venus Project proposes the building of a new, experimental city, the purpose of which is:

1. To be a laboratory to test the validity of the project's designs and proposals.
2. To establish a permanent center that could be used for future long and short-term planning.

The circular configurations of these new cities proposed by *The Venus Project* are not just stylized, architectural conceptualizations, but the results of years of research into an environment that best serves the needs of the occupants efficiently and economically. Without sufficient knowledge of the symbiotic interrelationship between humanity and the environment, it would be extremely difficult to develop workable solutions to our many problems. *The Venus Project* has taken this and many other factors into careful consideration and study.

This new experimental city would be devoted to working towards the aims and goals of *The Venus Project*, which are:

1.   Realizing the declaration of the world's resources as being the common heritage of all the earth's people.
2.   Transcending the need for the artificial boundaries that currently and arbitrarily separate people.
3.   Replacing the monetary-based economy with a resource-based world economy.
4.   Assisting in stabilizing the world's population through education and voluntary birth control.
5.   Reclaiming and restoring the natural environment to the best of our ability.
6.   Redesigning our cities, transportation systems, and agricultural and industrial plants so that they are energy efficient, clean, and able to conveniently serve the needs of all people.
7.   Gradually outgrowing the need for corporate entities and governments (whether local, national, or supra-national) as a means of social management.
8.   Sharing and applying new technologies for the benefit of all nations.
9.   Developing and using clean, renewable energy sources.
10.   Manufacturing the highest quality products for the benefit of the world's people.

11. Requiring environmental impact studies prior to construction of any mega projects.

12. Encouraging the widest range of creativity and incentive toward constructive endeavor.

13. Outgrowing nationalism, bigotry and prejudice through education.

14. Eliminating any type of elitism, technical or otherwise.

15. Arriving at methodologies by careful research rather than random opinions.

16. Enhancing communication in schools so that our language is relevant to the physical conditions of the world.

17. Providing not only the necessities of life, but also offering challenges that stimulate the mind while emphasizing individuality rather than uniformity.

18. Finally, preparing people intellectually and emotionally for the changes and challenges that lie ahead.

Like all innovative social proposals, ours starts with a few devoted people who dedicate their time to informing others of the humane benefits of this new direction and to a variety of tasks pertinent to the project. All people are invited to participate in whatever capacity they can, to help carry out the initial design phases of this new experimental city. During the initial phase, we will utilize an interdisciplinary team of systems analysts, engineers, computer programmers, architects, city planners, sociologists, psychologists, educators, etc.

The design of *The Venus Project* does not regard environmental conditions as fixed or static. We must allow for adaptation and change as a continuous process. This avoids the tendency to perpetuate temporary arrangements beyond their period of usefulness.

A circular city would be a transitional phase and could evolve from a semi-cooperative, money-oriented society to a resource-based economy. This could be the prototype for a series of cities to be constructed in various places throughout the world. The rate of progression will depend upon the availability of funds raised during the early stages and the people who identify with, participate in, and support the aims and direction of *The Venus Project*.

As these new communities develop and become more widely accepted, they may very well form the basis of a new civilization, preferably through the process of evolution rather than revolution.

We are well aware no one can actually foretell the shape of the future. We can only extrapolate on present information and trends. Population growth, technological change, worldwide environmental conditions, and available resources are the primary criteria for future projections.

We are also aware that there is no single philosophy or point of view — religious, political, scientific, or ideological — that someone would not be able to take issue with. We feel certain, however, that the only aspects of *The Venus Project* that may appear threatening are those which others project onto it.

The Venus Project is neither Utopian nor Orwellian, nor does it reflect the dreams of impractical idealists. Instead, it presents attainable goals requiring only the intelligent application of what we already know. The only limitations are those which we impose upon ourselves.

The Venus Project does not advocate any type of sabotage of the existing free-enterprise system. We believe that it will come to an end of its own accord, as indicated in this book. We do, however, wish to provide an alternative approach for your consideration. We encourage you to become better informed about the proposals of this project through our books, videos and seminars. If you identify with this direction, we welcome you to join with us and work towards its realization.

A view from space presents us with an ever-changing image of this beautiful planet, an impression that our world is one. The artificial, national borderlines do not appear. We are finally beginning to realize that humankind is but one single family. Only when the nations of the world can agree upon a common direction and can state the problems precisely, will we be able to reach workable solutions. In times to come, the need for all forms of loyalties and beliefs that divide, mislead, and destroy social continuity should vanish, and we may realize that most of the major problems confronting the nations of the world are human in origin. We must act, and act swiftly, to avoid further degradation of both our planet and ourselves. We must act while both the earth and humankind still retain their intrinsic worth.

TO CLOSE, WE INVITE YOUR COMMENTS AND PARTICIPATION.

In the spirit of Angeles Philolias:

"In the final analysis:
We are one people — we share one Planet.
We wish to live in Peace and heal the Earth.
We will do our best to make this a reality.
We will change what needs changing based upon loving, sharing, and serving all humanity.
We, the people of Earth, are one family."

FOR FURTHER INFORMATION PLEASE CONTACT:

The Venus Project
21 Valley Lane
Venus, FL 33960
U.S.A.

Phone: 863-465-0321
Fax: 863-465-1928
http://www.thevenusproject.com
tvp@thevenusproject.com

FOR FURTHER INFORMATION

VIDEOS

WELCOME TO THE FUTURE

It is an overview explanation of the direction and the aims of The Venus Project. This video presents an attainable vision of what our world could be if we intelligently apply science and technology with environmental and human concern — a future where war, poverty and hunger could be but a distant memory. It advocates surpassing the monetary system by introducing a resource-based economy, in which all of the world's resources are utilized for the common heritage of all people. It presents a vision of future cities (on land and sea), new architecture, silent and efficient transportation, clean energy alternatives, The Venus Project's 25-acre design and research center and much more. Included are interviews with project founder and director, Jacque Fresco, his assistant Roxanne Meadows and others.

A **STUDY GUIDE** is included with this video. Structured in three sections. *Running time approximately 53 minutes.*

Price $29.95 plus S&H

THE VENUS PROJECT: THE REDESIGN OF A CIULTURE

This introductory video of The Venus Project presents a future that is attainable today. It shows a view of the wonderful choices and limitless possibilities in The Venus Project: a bold new direction for humanity.
Running time approximately 20 minutes.

Price $ 18.95 plus S&H

CITIES IN THE SEA

This video takes one on a journey of tomorrow's cities in the sea. It presents Jacque Fresco's fantastic and imaginative designs and footage of numerous massive ocean structures that will monitor and protect the ocean environment while providing recreation, education and an enriching lifestyle for the occupants. This can be accomplished with the utmost concern for the marine environment and energy efficient systems.
Running time approximately 15 minutes.

Price $19.95 & S&H

163

BOOKS

THE BEST THAT MONEY CAN'T BUY: BEYOND POLITICS, POVERTY, & WAR

Published in 2001, 170 pages, softcover. Hundreds of books address technological change, business process management, human productivity, and environmental issues. Almost all overlook the major element in all these systems — human beings and their social structures and culture. This book offers a possible alternative and methods to consciously fuse all these elements to create a sustainable future for all our planetary inhabitants, as well as fundamental changes in the way we regard ourselves, one another and our world. 70 color photos of Fresco's original designs representing this possible future are also presented.

Price $24.95 & S&H

THE VENUS PROJECT: THE REDESIGN OF A CULTURE

Published in 1995, 56 pages, softcover. This book gives the reader an introductory overview of *The Venus Project's* aims and proposals. The informative text is accompanied by 70 wonderful color and B&W photos and illustrations of many of *The Venus Project's* futuristic designs and concepts, as well as the existing 25-acre design and research facility. This book is sure to provide the reader with not only a graphic visualization of the possibilities for a better tomorrow, but also with a sense of hope for the future of humankind in our technological age.

Price $18.95 & S&H

LECTURES AND SEMINARS

Jacque Fresco is available for lectures and seminars.

ORDER THROUGH OUR WEBSITE OR CONTACT:

THE VENUS PROJECT
Roxanne Meadows
21 Valley Lane
Venus, Fl 33960

Phone: 863-465-0321
Fax: 863-465-1928
e-mail: tvp@thevenusproject.com
www.thevenusproject.com